GOSPEL PLAYS FOR STUDENTS

GOSPEL PLAYS
FOR STUDENTS

36 Scripts for Education and Worship

Sr. Mary Kathleen Glavich, SND

TWENTY-THIRD PUBLICATIONS
Mystic, Connecticut

Acknowledgments

I am grateful to Sister Mary Joell Overman, S.N.D., Sister Rita Mary Harwood, S.N.D., Sister Mary Nathan Hess, S.N.D., and to the many other Sisters in my community who have encouraged and supported me in my writing ministry.

My appreciation, too, to the kind and helpful personnel at Twenty-Third Publications who have made this book a reality.

Excerpts taken from *The New American Bible* with Revised New Testament, Copyright ©1986 by the Confraternity of Christian Doctrine, Washington, D.C. are used with permission. All rights reserved.

The biblical art by Helen Siegl in this volume is from *Clip-Art for Feasts and Seasons* © 1984, Pueblo Publishing Company. All rights reserved. Used with permission.

Twenty-Third Publications
185 Willow Street
P.O. Box 180
Mystic, CT 06355
(203) 536-2611

Library of Congress Catalog Number 89-50562
ISBN 0-89622-407-4

Contents

Dedicated to the Most Reverend Anthony M. Pilla
Bishop of Cleveland
in gratitude for his wholehearted and courageous
leadership

GOSPEL PLAYS FOR STUDENTS

INTRODUCTION

Gospel Plays for Students: 36 Scripts for Education and Worship is a companion to *Acting Out the Miracles and Parables: 52 Five-Minute Plays for Education and Worship.* It contains thirty-six gospel accounts of events from the life of Jesus in playlet form. It is intended to supplement the regular religion program. The playlets can be incorporated into lessons on related topics. They are an alternative to having the students read the textbook, read the Bible, or produce their own plays. Granted that student-created plays are interesting, fun, and effective learning activities, but prepared scripts are more accurate and less time consuming.

These brief plays can be used in the context of a lesson as
* a lively introduction
* a method of developing a Bible story
* a review activity
* a culminating activity
* a lead into a prayer experience.

They can be presented
* for another class or other group
* as part of a program for parents and other guests
* within a liturgical or paraliturgical service.

The playlets are adaptable to any grade level for several reasons. The gospel stories themselves are simple and so is their vocabulary. Most of them are familiar. Furthermore, the lessons of the basic religion text provide the necessary preparation and follow-up that make the playlets consonant with the students' developmental stage.

Most of the wording of the playlets is based on the 1986 edition of *The New American Bible.* Those playlets for events that appear in more than one gospel account are a blend of the versions. Where dialogue is described in the Scriptures or merely implied, it has been supplied.

Each playlet in this book is on a separate page so that copies can be easily duplicated for the actors and for others involved in staging the playlets. Cast names marked + in the Director's Handbook can be adjusted to the size of the class to allow as many students as possible to participate.

Catechists, especially novice producers and directors, should not miss the feature "Tips for Putting on Playlets" on page 70. The ten suggestions there are very important for smooth performances that are rewarding for all.

There are two features in the Director's Handbook to help catechists plan when each playlet would be most appropriate for presentation. The first is a chart on pages 93-94 of those Sunday or feast-day gospels in each liturgical cycle that are about a gospel event in this book. This is for ease in preparing for Sunday or feast-day liturgies that may be enhanced by a playlet. The second feature is a topical index listing the events in this book according to theme in order to assist in correlating the playlets with the year's curriculum.

The Director's Handbook prepares catechists to use the playlets. Each gospel event is explained briefly under Comments. These notes clarify what happened, supply background information for better understanding of the event, and indicate its significance. In addition, topics for discussion are suggested for each playlet. Some of these points focus on the main message of the Scripture passage. Others are meant to reveal the meaning of concepts that students might find puzzling or might overlook. Most important, some points lead the student to relate the events to themselves and their world.

Gospel Plays for Students should be a help to all catechists who regard variety and student involvement as essential ingredients of a good lesson. Its ready-made playlets will enable us to teach creatively without undue time spent preparing plays. In addition, our students will encounter the Scriptures and Jesus in an enjoyable way: through an experience they will remember more than reading a page in a book.

The Announcement of John's Birth

Luke 1:5-25

(Zechariah kneels before table with incense. Persons 1, 2, 3 kneel praying at a distance.)

Narrator
Zechariah was a priest. He and his wife Elizabeth were good, holy people. They were very old and never had any children. One day Zechariah was chosen by lot to burn incense in the Temple.

(Angel Gabriel enters and stands at right of altar. Zechariah gasps and trembles.)

Angel
Do not be afraid, Zechariah, because your prayer has been heard. Your wife Elizabeth will bear you a son, and you shall name him John. And you will have joy and gladness, and many will rejoice at his birth, for he will be great in the sight of the Lord.
    He will drink neither wine nor strong drink. He will be filled with the Holy Spirit, and he will turn many of the children of Israel to the Lord their God. He will prepare a people fit for the Lord.

Zechariah
How shall I know this? For I am an old man, and my wife is an old woman.

Angel
I am Gabriel, who stands before God. I was sent to speak to you and to announce to you this good news. But now you will be unable to talk until the day these things take place, because you did not believe my words. *(Angel exits.)*

Person 1
What's taking Zechariah so long? He should be finished by now.

Person 2
Maybe he's ill. He's pretty old.

(Zechariah rises and walks slowly in a daze toward the people.)

Person 1
Here he comes.

3

(Zechariah gestures to the place he left and to his mouth. He points to heaven.)

Person 3   Why doesn't he speak?

Person 2   I think he's had a vision.

(All exit.)

The Annunciation

Luke 1:26-38

(Mary is walking on the stage.)

Narrator   In the sixth month, the angel Gabriel was sent from God to a town of Galilee called Nazareth, to a virgin betrothed to a man named Joseph, of the house of David. And the virgin's name was Mary.

(Gabriel enters and goes to Mary. Mary gasps.)

Gabriel   Hail, favored one! The Lord is with you.

(Mary puts her hand over her heart and looks frightened.)

Gabriel   Do not be afraid, Mary, for you have found favor with God. Behold, you will conceive in your womb and bear a son, and you shall name him Jesus. He will be great and will be called Son of the Most High. The Lord God will give him the throne of David, his father. He will rule over the house of Jacob forever, and of his kingdom there will be no end.

Mary   How can this be, since I have no relations with a man?

Gabriel   The Holy Spirit will come upon you, and the power of the Most High will overshadow you. Therefore the child to be born will be called holy, the Son of God. And behold, Elizabeth, your relative, has also conceived a son in her old age. This is the sixth month for her who was called barren. For nothing will be impossible for God.

Mary   *(bowing)* Behold, I am the handmaid of the Lord. May it be done to me according to your word.

(Gabriel exits.)

The Visitation

Luke 1:39-56

(Elizabeth is stirring a pot or sweeping the floor.)

Narrator After the angel appeared to her, Mary set out and traveled to the hill country in haste to a town of Judah. She was going help her elderly relative Elizabeth, who was pregnant.

(Mary enters and goes quickly toward Elizabeth. She pretends to open a door and steps inside.)

Mary Elizabeth! How are you?

Elizabeth *(surprised)* Ah! *(Puts her hand on her stomach)* . . . Mary!

(Mary and Elizabeth hug each other.)

Elizabeth Most blessed are you among women, and blessed is the fruit of your womb. And how does this happen to me, that the mother of my Lord should come to me? For at the moment the sound of your greeting reached my ears, the infant in my womb leaped for joy. Blessed are you who believed that what was spoken to you by the Lord would be fulfilled.

Mary My soul proclaims the greatness of the Lord.
My spirit rejoices in God my savior.
For he has looked upon his handmaid's lowliness.
Behold, from now on all ages will call me blessed.
The Mighty One has done great things for me,
   and holy is his name.
His mercy is from age to age
   to those who fear him.
He has shown might with his arm and
   scattered the proud.
He has thrown down rulers from their thrones
   but lifted up the lowly.
The hungry he has filled with good things.
   The rich he has sent away empty.

He has helped Israel his servant,
  remembering his mercy,
according to his promise to our fathers,
  to Abraham and to his descendants forever.

Elizabeth   Zechariah will be home soon. He can't speak, you know, ever since he found out about our baby. He'll be glad to see you, too! How long can you stay?

Mary   About three months.

Elizabeth   Wonderful! Now tell me about yourself and the great things the Lord has done for you.

(Mary and Elizabeth sit down.)

Narrator   Mary helped Elizabeth during the last months of her pregnancy. Then she returned home to prepare for her own child.

BLEST IS THE FRUIT OF YOUR WOMB LK 1·42

The Birth of John
Luke 1:57-78

Narrator   When Elizabeth and her husband Zechariah were very old, she became pregnant and bore a son. She was no longer ashamed for being childless, and she thanked God. Eight days after her son was born, neighbors and relatives came for a Jewish celebration.

(Zechariah, Elizabeth carrying a baby, and Persons 1, 2, 3 enter.)

Person 1   Let's name him Zechariah.

Person 2   Yes, he should be named after his father.

Elizabeth   No. He will be called John.

Person 3   None of your relatives has this name.

(Persons 1, 2, 3 turn to Zechariah, point to baby, and raise their hands questioningly.)

(Zechariah motions as if writing and extends his hand. Person 2 brings him pencil and paper. Zechariah writes. Person 1 looks over his shoulder.)

Person 1   He wrote, "John is his name."

Person 3   I don't believe it.   How strange.

Zechariah   Blessed be God!

Person 2   He can speak now!

Person 1   What can this mean?

Person 3   Let's get out of here.

Person 2   What will this child be?

Zechariah   Blessed be the Lord, the God of Israel,
     for he has visited and brought redemption to his people.
(holding up baby) And you, child, will be called
prophet of the Most High,
     for you will go before the Lord to prepare his ways,
to give his people knowledge of salvation
     through the forgiveness of their sins,
because of the tender mercy of our God.

Narrator   The child of Zechariah and Elizabeth was John the Baptist, the great prophet who prepared the people for Jesus.

The Birth of Jesus
Luke 2:1-20

(Shepherds are on one side of the stage. Half are sleeping. Innkeeper is on stage, writing on a scroll.)

Narrator   In those days a decree went out from Caesar Augustus that the whole world should be enrolled. This was the first census, when Quirinius was governor of Syria. So all went to be enrolled, each to his own town. And Joseph, too, went up from Galilee from the town of Nazareth to Judea, to the city of David that is called Bethlehem, because he was of the house and family of David, to be enrolled with Mary, his betrothed, who was with child.

(Mary and Joseph enter, walking slowly. They stop at "door" and Joseph knocks. Innkeeper goes to door.)

Innkeeper   Yes?

Joseph   Would you have room for two, my wife and me?

Innkeeper   Sorry, but the house is filled.

Joseph   We'd appreciate even a small space. My wife is expecting any day.

Innkeeper   *(shaking head)* Sorry. Wish I could help. Wait. There's the stable in the back.

Joseph   That would be fine.

Innkeeper   Come with me.

(Mary and Joseph enter and go to the back with the Innkeeper. Joseph helps Mary to a chair.)

Joseph   *(to Innkeeper)* Thank you, sir.

Innkeeper   Good night. *(Exits.)*

Mary   It's almost time, Joseph.

10

(While Narrator speaks, Joseph, with his back to the audience, takes the doll and cloths from the basket. He gives them to Mary. She wraps the doll in the cloths and sets it in the manger.)

Narrator   While they were there, the time came for Mary to have her child, and she gave birth to her firstborn son. She wrapped him in swaddling clothes and laid him in a manger.

(Angel 1 enters and stands before the Shepherds. Shepherds gasp and shield their faces. The sleeping ones awake and rub their eyes.)

Angel 1   Do not be afraid. Behold, I proclaim to you good news of great joy that will be for all the people. For today in the city of David a savior has been born for you who is Messiah and Lord. And this will be a sign for you: You will find an infant wrapped in swaddling clothes and lying in a manger.

(Angels enter and join Angel 1.)

Angels   Glory to God in the highest and on earth peace to those on whom his favor rests.
(Angels exit.)

THEY WENT FROM NAZARETH TO BETHLEHEM LK2.4

(Angels exit.)

Shepherd 1   *(to Shepherd 2)*   Let us go, then, to Bethlehem to see this thing that has taken place, which the Lord has made known to us.

(Shepherds run to Mary and Joseph.)

Shepherd 2   *(to Mary and Joseph)*   We have come to see the infant. Angels told us about the savior.

(Mary and Joseph gesture to manger. Shepherds kneel around it. Shepherds rise. Shepherds exit except for Shepherd 1. Man enters.)

Shepherd 1   *(going to Man)*   A wonderful thing has happened. We were watching our flocks, and angels appeared and told us that a savior was born in Bethlehem. They said we would find him in a manger. We went to Bethlehem and found the baby and his parents just as the angels said.

Man   Amazing! Tell me more.

(Shepherd 1 and Man exit.)

The Visit of the Magi

Matthew 2:1-12

(Priest 1 and Scribe 1 are on stage. Magi enter.)

Narrator   When Jesus was born in Bethlehem of Judea, in the days of King Herod, behold, Magi, wise men from the east, arrived in Jerusalem.

(Magi enter and go to Priest 1 and Scribe 1.)

Magi 1   Where is the newborn king of the Jews?

Magi 2   We saw his star at its rising and have come to do him homage.

Priest 1   I don't know anything about him.

(Magi exit.)

Priest 1   *(to Scribe 1)*   We'd better tell King Herod about this.

(Priest 1 and Scribe 1 exit.)

Narrator   When King Herod was told, he was greatly troubled, and all Jerusalem was, too.

(King Herod, Priest 1, and Scribe 1 enter.)

King Herod   Have all the chief priests and the scribes come here.

Priest 1   Yes, your Highness.

(Priest 1 and Scribe 1 exit. Priests and Scribes enter and stand before King Herod. Messenger enters and stands in back.)

King Herod   Tell me, where is the Messiah to be born?

Priest 2   In Bethlehem of Judea.

Scribe 2   For the prophet wrote, "And you, Bethlehem, land of Judah, are by no means least among the rulers of Judah.

From you shall come a ruler, who is to shepherd my people Israel."

King Herod   Go. That's all I wanted to know.

(All exit except Messenger.)

King Herod   *(to Messenger)*   Come here.

(Messenger goes to King Herod.)

King Herod   Find those Magi from the east and have them come here. Don't let anyone know I sent you.

Messenger   Yes, your Highness. *(Messenger exits.)*

Herod   *(pacing back and forth)* A new king! I must get rid of him.

(Messenger and Magi enter.)

King Herod	*(to Magi)* Thank you for coming. Naturally I'm interested in the new king. When did you see the star appear?
Narrator	Herod learned about the star from the Magi.
King Herod	Go and search carefully for the child. When you have found him, bring me word, that I too may go and do him homage.
Magi 1	We'll be glad to.
	(Magi bow, and King Herod and Messenger exit. Magi walk a little way.)
Magi 3	*(excitedly)* Look! There's the star again!
Magi 1	It's moving ahead of us.
Magi 2	To guide us to the newborn king.
	(Mary enters with child and sits in the background. Magi continue to walk.)
Magi 1	It stopped moving.
Magi 2	It's right above this house. Let's go in. *(Magi go to Mary and kneel down.)*
Magi 3	Hail, king of the Jews!
Magi 2	We bring you gifts from our country.
	(Magi present gold, frankincense, and myrrh. Mary smiles and accepts them.)
Narrator	The Magi were warned in a dream not to return to Herod, so they went back to their country by another way. When Herod realized that he had been tricked by the Magi, he was very angry. He had all boys two years and under who lived in and around Bethlehem killed. But Mary, Joseph, and Jesus escaped to Egypt.

15

The Presentation

Luke 2:22-38

(Mary and Joseph enter. Joseph carries the birds, and Mary holds the baby.)

Narrator   It was a Jewish law that every boy should be offered to God soon after birth and that a lamb or two birds be sacrificed. Mary and Joseph brought Jesus to Jerusalem to present him to the Lord. A holy man named Simeon was waiting for the savior of Israel. The Holy Spirit let him know that he would not die until he had seen the Messiah of the Lord. The day Mary and Joseph came to the Temple Simeon was led there by the Spirit.

THEY BROUGHT HIM TO JERUSALEM TO PRESENT HIM TO THE LORD · LK 2·22

(Simeon enters, goes to Mary and Joseph, and takes the baby into his arms.)

Simeon   Blessed be the God of Israel!
Now, Master, you may let your servant go
    in peace, according to your word,

for my eyes have seen your salvation,
    which you prepared in sight of all the people,
a light for revelation to the Gentiles,
    and glory for your people Israel.

Mary   How amazing!

Joseph   Remarkable!

(Simeon puts his hand on Mary's and Joseph's heads.)

Simeon   May God bless you both. *(turning to Mary)* Behold, this child is destined for the fall and rise of many in Israel. He is to be a sign that will be contradicted, and you yourself a sword will pierce, so that the thoughts of many hearts may be revealed. *(Places baby in Mary's arms.)*

Narrator   Anna, a prophetess, was eighty-four years old. She had moved into the Temple long ago when her husband died. She never left the Temple but fasted and prayed night and day.

(Anna enters and goes to Mary and Joseph.)

Anna   Thanks be to God! May I hold him?

(Mary gives Anna the baby.)

Anna   Wait until the others hear. They will be so glad that our redeemer has come.

Narrator   Simeon and Anna were faithful to God. They were rewarded by seeing the Messiah they had longed for.

The Boy Jesus in the Temple
Luke 2:41-52

(Jesus is seated on a chair off to the side. Teachers are seated around him.)

Narrator   Jewish people went to Jerusalem every year for the feast of Passover. Each year Mary and Joseph went, too. When Jesus was twelve years old, they went to Jerusalem according to the custom. On the way home, Mary and Joseph missed Jesus.

(Joseph enters. Mary enters a little later.)

Mary   Joseph, isn't Jesus with you?

Joseph   No, Mary. I haven't seen him since we left. He's probably with his cousins. He's somewhere in this caravan.

Mary   Let's look for him.

(Relatives 1 and 2 enter.)

Mary   *(to Relative 1)* Have you seen Jesus?

Relative 1   No, not all day.

Joseph   *(to Relative 2)* We're looking for our son. Has he been with you?

Relative 2   No, sorry. I haven't seen him. Let me ask John. *(Calls.)* John, come here a minute.

(John enters and goes to Relative 2.)

Relative 2   *(to John)* Son, Joseph here is looking for Jesus. Was he playing with you and the others today?

John   No, Dad. He wasn't with us.

Mary   *(to Joseph)* Joseph, I'm frightened. We better go back to Jerusalem to look for him.

(Relatives and John exit. Mary and Joseph walk around.)

Narrator   Mary and Joseph searched for Jesus all over Jerusalem. After three days they found him in the Temple sitting in the midst of the teachers.

Teacher 1   *(to Jesus)*   Yahweh is a mighty God.

Teacher 2   Yes. We must follow his commands carefully.

Jesus   True, but is it better to serve out of fear or out of love?

Teacher 1   *(to Teacher 2)*   How can one so young be so wise?

(Mary and Joseph see Jesus and go to him.)

Mary   *(to Joseph)*   Look. He's with the teachers. It sounds as if he is teaching *them.*

Joseph   I don't know what to say!

Mary   (to Jesus) Son, why have you done this to us? Your father and I have been looking for you, worried to death.

Jesus   Did you not know that I must be in my Father's house?

        (Mary and Joseph look at each other.)

Joseph (to Mary) What does that mean?

Mary   I don't know.

Joseph (taking Jesus by the arm) It's time we went home, Son. Let's go.

Narrator   Jesus went with them to Nazareth and was obedient to them. Mary kept all these things in her heart. And Jesus grew in wisdom and age and favor before God and people.

The Baptism of Jesus

Matthew 3:4-17   Mark 1:4-11   Luke 3: 7-22   John 1:19-34

(John is facing Crowd. Person and Priest are in the Crowd.)

Narrator   John the Baptist preached in the desert of Judea. He wore clothing made of camel's hair and a leather belt. He ate locusts and wild honey. All the people in the region were being baptized by John in the Jordan River as they admitted their sins.

John   Every tree that does not bear good fruit will be cut down and thrown into the fire.

Person   What should we do?

John   Whoever has two cloaks should share with the person who has none. And whoever has food should also share.

Priest   Who are you?

John   I am not the Messiah. I am the voice of one crying out in the desert, "Make straight the way of the Lord."

Person   I am a sinner. But I am sorry. Please baptize me.

(Person "wades" to John. John pours water on Person.)

John   I baptize with water, but there is one mightier than I who is coming. I am not worthy to untie his sandal strap. He will baptize you with the Holy Spirit and fire.

Narrator   One day Jesus came from Galilee to John at the Jordan River to be baptized.

(Jesus enters and goes to John.)

John   *(surprised)*   I need to be baptized by *you*, and yet you are coming to me?

Jesus   Allow it now, for it is fitting to fulfill the plan.

(Jesus "wades" into the water toward John. John pours water over his head.)

Narrator   Suddenly the heavens were opened, and the Spirit of God came down like a dove upon him.

(Jesus looks up.)

Voice   This is my beloved Son, with whom I am well pleased.

Narrator   With his baptism, Jesus accepted his mission and was filled with power to begin it.

JESUS WAS BAPTIZED IN THE JORDAN BY JOHN MK1·9

The Temptation of Jesus

Matthew 4:1-11   Mark 1:12-13   Luke 4:1-13

(Jesus kneels, praying.)

Narrator   After his baptism, Jesus was led by the Spirit into the desert for forty days. He ate nothing during those days and was very hungry.

(Devil enters and goes to Jesus. Jesus looks surprised.)

THE DEVIL SHOWED HIM ALL THE KINGDOMS OF THE WORLD · LK 4·5

Devil   *(picking up rock)*   If you are the Son of God, command these stones to become loaves of bread.

Jesus   *(in a strong voice)*   It is written, "One does not live by bread alone, but by every word that comes forth from the mouth of God."

Devil   Come with me.

Narrator   The devil took Jesus to the Temple in the holy city and made him stand on the edge of the roof.

(Devil and Jesus stand on chairs.)

Devil   If you are the Son of God, throw yourself down. For it is written, "He will command his angels to guard you," and "With their hands they will support you lest you dash your foot against a stone."

Jesus   *(with a strong voice)*   Again it is written, "You shall not put the Lord, your God, to the test."

(Devil makes a disappointed gesture. The Devil and Jesus step off chairs and walk around.)

Narrator   Next the devil took Jesus up to a very high mountain.

(Devil and Jesus climb chairs.)

Devil   Look at all these kingdoms of the world. Look at their magnificence. All these I shall give to you, if you worship me.

Jesus   *(shouting and pointing)*   Get away, Satan! It is written, "The Lord, your God, shall you worship and him alone shall you serve."

(Devil exits angrily.)

Narrator   Angels came and waited on Jesus.

(Angels enter and bow before Jesus.)

The First Apostles

John 1:35-51

(John, Andrew, and Disciple are talking together.)

Narrator   One day John was with two of his disciples.

(Jesus enters and walks by. John stops talking and watches Jesus pass.)

John   *(gesturing toward Jesus)* Behold, the Lamb of God.

(Andrew and Disciple wave to John and run after Jesus. They follow him a while.)

Jesus   *(turning)*   What are you looking for?

(Andrew and Disciple look at each other.)

Andrew   Rabbi. . .

Disciple   Teacher, where are you staying?

Jesus   *(laughing)*   Come, and you will see.

(Jesus, Andrew, and Disciple walk on for a while, then sit at the table.)

Narrator   They stayed with Jesus that day. It was about 4:00 in the afternoon.

(Andrew and Disciple rise, wave, and leave. Jesus stands. Simon Peter enters. Andrew runs to him. Jesus sits.)

Andrew   Here you are. We have found the Messiah. Come on. You have to meet him.

(Andrew grabs Simon Peter by the arm and they walk to Jesus. Jesus rises.)

Andrew   Jesus, this is my brother Simon.

(Jesus and Simon shake hands.)

Jesus   *(looking into Simon's eyes)*   You are Simon, the son of John. You will be called Peter.

(All exit.)

Narrator   The next day Jesus decided to go to Galilee. He found Philip who lived in Bethsaida where Andrew and Peter lived.

(Jesus enters from one side and Philip from another. Nathanael enters and stands at a distance under the tree.)

Jesus   *(to Philip as they pass each other)*   Follow me.

(Philip turns around and walks with Jesus for a while.)

Philip   I'll see you later.

(Philip leaves Jesus and goes to Nathanael. Jesus sits down.)

Philip   *(to Nathanael)*   We have found the one about whom Moses wrote in the law, and also the prophets. He is Jesus, son of Joseph, from Nazareth.

Nathanael   Can anything good come from Nazareth?

Philip   Come and see.

(Philip and Nathanael approach Jesus.)

Jesus   Here is a true Israelite. There is no falseness in him.

Nathanael   How do you know me?

Jesus   *(rising)* Before Philip called you, I saw you under the fig tree.

Nathanael   Rabbi, you are the Son of God. You are the King of Israel.

Jesus   Do you believe because I told you that I saw you under the fig tree? You will see greater things than this. Amen, amen, I say to you, you will see the sky opened and the angels of God ascending and descending on the Son of Man.

(All exit.)

The Call of the First Apostles

Matthew 4:18-22   Mark 1:16-20

(Peter and Andrew are in one boat. James, John, Zebedee, and Hired Men 1, 2 are mending nets in the other boat some distance away.)

Narrator   The brothers Peter and Andrew were fishing one day. The brothers James and John were with their father Zebedee and some hired men mending their nets.

(Jesus enters. Peter and Andrew cast a net into the sea while Jesus watches.)

Jesus   *(calling to Peter and Andrew)*   Come after me, and I will make you fishers of men.

(Jesus walks on. Peter and Andrew jump out of boat and catch up to Jesus. They all walk over to the other boat.)

Jesus   *(shouting)*   James. John. Come after me, and I will make you fishers of men.

(James and John get out of boat, wave to Zebedee, and follow Jesus. Zebedee waves back.)

Narrator   All the fishermen Jesus called went off in his company, leaving their jobs and their homes.

THEY IMMEDIATELY ABANDONED THEIR
NETS AND BECAME HIS FOLLOWERS · MK 1·18

The Call of Matthew

Matthew 9:9:13   Mark 2:14-17   Luke 5:27-32

(Matthew sits behind table.)

Narrator   Matthew was a tax collector. Jewish people did not like Jewish men who collected taxes for their conquerer, Rome. Often these tax collectors kept some money for themselves. One day Matthew was sitting at the customs post.

(Jesus and Disciples enter. Jesus goes to Matthew.)

Jesus   *(to Matthew)* Follow me.

(Matthew stands and follows Jesus.)

Matthew   *(to Jesus)* Master, come to my house for dinner.

(All walk to other table. Sinners enter and sit with Jesus and Disciples. Pharisees enter and sit apart.)

Narrator   While Jesus was at table in Matthew's house, many tax collectors and sinners came and sat with Jesus and his disciples.

(Pharisees 1, 2 leave group and go to Disciples.)

Pharisee 1   *(to Disciple 1)*   Why does your teacher eat with tax collectors and sinners?

(Jesus looks up at Pharisees.)

Jesus   *(to Pharisees)*   Those who are well do not need a physician, but the sick do. Go and learn the meaning of the words, "I desire mercy, not sacrifice." I did not come to call the righteous, but sinners.

The Blessing of the Children

Matthew 19:13-15   Mark 10:13-16   Luke 18:15-17

(Jesus is seated. Disciples are around him. Mothers enter holding Children by the hand and carrying babies. They go to Jesus.)

Mother 1   Master, won't you bless my child?

Mother 2   Jesus, touch my baby.

Mother 3   Please pray over my son Jacob.

(Disciples shoo Mothers and Children away.)

Disciple 1   *(to Mothers)* Leave him alone.

Disciple 2   Can't you see how tired he is?

Jesus   *(beckoning to Children)* Come, children. *(scolding Disciples)* Let the children come to me. Do not stop them, for the kingdom of God belongs to such as these. Amen, I say to you, whoever does not accept the kingdom of God like a child will not enter it.

(Jesus takes a baby in his arms. He puts his hand on Child 1's head. Children surround him. Mothers smile at Disciples.)

WHOEVER WELCOMES A CHILD WELCOMES ME ✠ MK 9·37

The Cleansing of the Temple

Mark 11:15-18   Matthew 21:12-13   Luke 19:45-46   John 2:13-22

(Moneychangers are seated and Sellers of Doves are standing behind tables. Bags of coins and cord are on a table. Jesus and Disciples 1, 2 enter and slowly walk toward tables.)

Narrator   Since the feast of Passover was near, Jesus went to Jerusalem. In the temple area he found those who sold oxen, sheep, and doves. Moneychangers were also seated there.

(Jesus picks up cord and waves it in the air.)

Jesus   Out! Get out of here. *(Hits table with cord. Pushes table over so coins spill.)*

(Moneychangers, oxen, and sheep exit in fear.)

Jesus   *(to Sellers of Doves)* Take these out of here, and stop making my Father's house a marketplace.

(Sellers of Doves exit.)

Disciple 1   *(to Disciple 2)*   Remember, Scripture says, "Zeal for your house will consume me."

(Jewish Persons 1, 2 enter and go to Jesus.)

Jewish
Person 1   What sign can you show us for doing this?

Jesus   Destroy this temple and in three days I will raise it up.

Jewish
Person 2   This Temple has been under construction for forty-six years, and you will raise it up in three days?

Narrator   Jesus was speaking about the temple of his body. When he was raised from the dead, his disciples remembered that he had said this. They came to believe the Scriptures and the words Jesus had spoken.

The Rich Young Man

Mark 10:17-31 Matthew 19:16-26 Luke 18:18-27

(Jesus and Disciples 1, 2 walk along. Rich Man enters, runs up to Jesus and kneels before him.)

Rich Man   Good teacher, what must I do to inherit eternal life?

Jesus   Why do you call me good? No one is good but God alone. You know the commandments: "You shall not kill. You shall not commit adultery. You shall not steal. You shall not bear false witness. You shall not defraud. Honor your father and your mother."

Rich Man   Teacher, all of these I have observed from my youth.

(Jesus, looking at him lovingly, bends over and puts his hand on his shoulder.)

Jesus   You are lacking in one thing. Go, sell what you have, and give to the poor, and you will have treasure in heaven. Then come, follow me.

(Rich Man lowers his head down, shaking it.   He rises and walks away from Jesus. Jesus watches sadly.)

Jesus   *(looking around at Disciples)*   How hard it is for those who have wealth to enter the kingdom of God.

Disciple 1   What marvelous teaching!

Disciple 2   Amazing!

Jesus   Children, how hard it is to enter the kingdom of God. It is easier for a camel to pass through the eye of a needle than for one who is rich to enter the kingdom of God.

Disciple 1   *(to Disciple 2)*   Then who can be saved?

Jesus   For human beings it is impossible, but not for God.

The Withered Fig Tree
Mark 11:12-14; 20-25   Matthew 21:18-22

(Jesus and Disciples walk along.)

Narrator   One day Jesus and his disciples were leaving Bethany.

Jesus   I'm hungry. Ah, I see a fig tree.

(Jesus leaves Disciples and goes ahead to the fig tree. He looks for figs.)

Jesus   There's nothing here but leaves. No fruit.

Disciple 1   *(to Disciple 2)*   But it's not the season for figs.

Jesus   *(to tree)* May no one ever eat of your fruit again!

(Jesus and Disciples exit.)

Narrator   Leaving Jerusalem early in the morning, Jesus and the disciples were walking along.

(Jesus and Disciples enter.)

Peter   Rabbi, look! The fig tree that you cursed has withered.

Jesus   Have faith in God. Amen, I say to you, whoever says to this mountain, "Be lifted up and thrown into the sea," and does not doubt in his heart but believes that what he says will happen, it shall be done for him. I tell you, all that you ask for in prayer, believe that you will receive it. It shall be yours.
    When you stand to pray, forgive anyone who has hurt you, so that your heavenly Father may in turn forgive you your sins.

The Samaritan Woman
John 4:4-42

Narrator Passing through Samaria Jesus and the disciples came to a town called Sychar. It was near the land Jacob had given to his son Joseph. Jacob's well was there. The Jewish people and the Samaritans did not get along. They would have nothing to do with each other.

(Jesus and Disciples enter. Jesus goes to chair and sits down.)

Jesus I'm tired from this journey. Let me sit a while here at Jacob's well.

Disciple 1 Sure, Master. We'll go into town and buy some food. *(to other Disciples)* Come on.

(Disciples exit. Woman enters with pail and goes to where Jesus is.)

Jesus Give me a drink.

Woman How can you, a Jew, ask me, a Samaritan woman, for a drink?

Jesus If you knew the gift of God and who is saying to you, "Give me a drink," you would have asked him and he would have given you living water.

Woman Sir, you do not even have a bucket and the well is deep. Where then can you get this living water? Are you greater than our father Jacob, who gave us this well and drank from it himself with his children and his flocks?

Jesus Everyone who drinks this water will be thirsty again. But whoever drinks the water I shall give will never thirst. The water I shall give will become in him a spring of water welling up to eternal life.

Woman Sir, give me this water, so that I may not be thirsty or have to keep coming here to draw water.

Jesus	Go call your husband and come back.
Woman	I do not have a husband.
Jesus	You are right in saying, "I do not have a husband." For you have had five husbands, and the one you have now is not your husband. What you have said is true.
Woman	Sir, I can see that you are a prophet. Our ancestors worshiped on this mountain. But your people say that the place to worship is in Jerusalem.
Jesus	Believe me, woman, the hour is coming when you will worship the Father neither on this mountain nor in Jerusalem. You people worship what you do not understand. We worship what we understand, because salvation is from the Jews. But the hour is coming, and is now here, when true worshipers will worship the Father in Spirit and truth. And indeed the Father seeks such people to worship him. God is Spirit, and those who worship him must worship in Spirit and truth.
Woman	I know that the Messiah is coming, the one called the Anointed. When he comes, he will tell us everything.
Jesus	I am he, the one who is speaking with you.
	(Disciples enter with package.)
Disciple 1	*(to Disciple 2)* Look. Jesus is talking to a woman.
Disciple 2	I don't believe my eyes!
	(Woman exits.)
Disciple 1	*(handing package to Jesus)* Rabbi, eat.
Jesus	I have food to eat of which you do not know.
Disciple 2	*(to Disciple 3)* Could someone have brought him something to eat?
Jesus	My food is to do the will of the one who sent me and to finish his work.

(Jesus opens package. Disciples sit down on the ground. Woman enters with Persons 1, 2.)

Woman   *(to Persons 1, 2)*   I'm sure he is the Messiah. He told me everything I have done.

Person 1   I believe you.

Person 2   I'll soon see if what you say is true.

(Woman and Persons 1, 2 go to Jesus.)

Woman   Rabbi, these are my neighbors.

Jesus   Glad to meet you.

Person 1   Won't you stay with us a while?

Jesus   I'd be happy to.

(All exit.)

Narrator   Jesus stayed with the Samaritans two days. Many more came to believe in him.

(All enter.)

Person 2   Jesus, we hate to see you go.

Person 1   Come again.

Jesus and Disciples   We'll try. So long. Thanks for everything.

(Jesus and Disciples exit, waving to Woman and Samaritans.)

Person 1   *(to Woman)* We no longer believe because of your word.

Person 2   We have heard for ourselves, and we know that this is truly the savior of the world.

The Pardon of the Sinful Woman
Luke 7:36-50

(Table and chairs are in the center. Simon and Persons 1, 2 are seated.)

Narrator   Once a Pharisee named Simon invited Jesus to dine with him.

(Jesus enters and goes to Simon.)

Jesus   Hello, Simon.

Simon   Jesus. I'm so glad you came. Welcome to my table.

(Jesus sits down.)

Simon   *(offering Jesus a plate)* Here, have some of this fresh bread.

Narrator   Now there was a sinful woman in the city who learned that Jesus was at table in the house of the Pharisee. She came with an alabaster flask of ointment.

(Woman enters with flask. She goes behind Jesus and weeps.)

Simon   Hey, you're getting his feet wet.

(Woman stoops and pretends to wipe Jesus' feet with her hair and kiss them.)

Person 1   *(to Person 2)* She's wiping his feet with her hair.

Person 2   And kissing them.

(Woman pretends to pour the flask of ointment on his feet.)

Simon   *(aside)* If this man were a prophet, he would know who and what sort of woman this is who is touching him. She is a sinner.

Jesus   Simon, I have something to say to you.

Simon   Tell me, teacher.

| Jesus | Two people were in debt to a certain man. One owed five hundred days' wages, and the other owed fifty. Since they were unable to repay the debt, he forgave it for both. Which of them will love him more? |

| Simon | I suppose the one who had a larger debt forgiven. |

| Jesus | You have judged rightly. |

| Jesus | *(turning and gesturing to Woman)* Do you see this woman? When I entered your house you did not give me water for my feet, but she has bathed them with her tears and wiped them with her hair. You did not give me a kiss, but she has not ceased kissing my feet since the time I entered. You did not anoint my head with oil, but she anointed my feet with ointment.
I tell you, her many sins have been forgiven, so she has shown great love. But the one to whom little is forgiven loves little. *(to Woman)* Your sins are forgiven. |

| Person 1 | *(to Person 2)* Who is this who even forgives sins? |

| Jesus | *(to Woman)* Your faith has saved you. Go in peace. |

(Woman exits.)

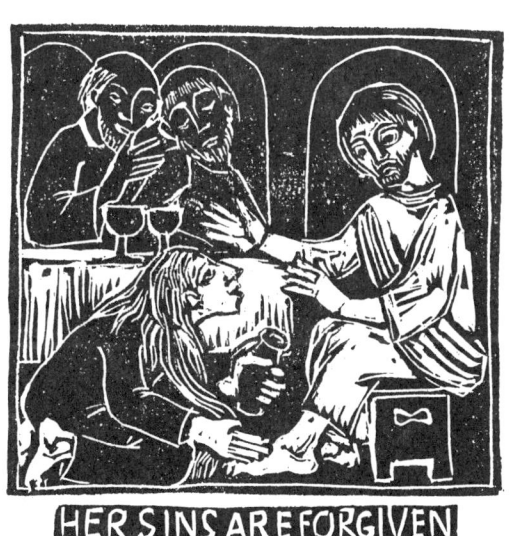

HER SINS ARE FORGIVEN
LK 7·47

The Anointing at Bethany

Matthew 26:6-13 Mark 14:3-9 John 12:1-8

(Jesus, Simon, and Persons 1, 2 are seated at table.)

Narrator One day Jesus was at table in the house of Simon the leper in Bethany. A woman came with an alabaster jar of costly perfumed oil.

(Woman enters. She "breaks" the top off the jar by hitting it against the table and pours the contents on Jesus' head.)

Person 1 *(angrily)* What a stupid thing to do!

Person 2 *(to Woman)* Why has there been this waste of perfumed oil?

Person 1 It could have been sold for more than three hundred days' wages.

Person 2 And the money given to the poor.

Jesus Let her alone. Why do you make trouble for her? She has done a good thing for me. The poor you will always have with you. Whenever you wish you can do good to them, but you will not always have me. *(gesturing toward Woman)* She has done what she could. By pouring this perfume upon my body, she has prepared me for burial.
    Amen, I say to you wherever the gospel is proclaimed to the whole world, what she has done will be told in memory of her.

Peter's Profession of Faith

Matthew 16:13-20   Mark 8:27-30   Luke 9:18-21

(Jesus, Peter, and Disciples 1, 2, 3 walk along.)

Jesus
Who do people say that the Son of Man is?

Disciple 1
Some say John the Baptist.

Disciple 2
Others, Elijah.

Disciple 3
Still others Jeremiah or one of the prophets.

(Jesus stops walking and faces the Disciples and Peter.)

Jesus
But who do *you* say that I am?

Peter
You are the Messiah, the Son of the living God.

(Jesus puts his hand on Peter's shoulder.)

Jesus
(to Peter)   Blessed are you, Simon son of John. For flesh and blood has not revealed this to you, but my heavenly Father.

And so I say to you, you are Peter, and upon this rock I will build my church, and the gates of the netherworld shall not prevail against it.

I will give you the keys to the kingdom of heaven. Whatever you bind on earth shall be bound in heaven; and whatever you loose on earth shall be loosed in heaven.

Jesus
(looking around at the Disciples) Now I give you strict orders: Don't tell anyone that I am the Messiah.

The Transfiguration of Jesus

Matthew 17:1-8   Mark 9:2-8   Luke 9:28-36

(Jesus, Peter, James, and John enter.)

Jesus   *(gesturing up)*   My three friends, come up this high mountain with me.

(Jesus, Peter, James, and John walk around with difficulty as if climbing.)

Narrator   Jesus and the three apostles went up the mountain by themselves. Jesus was transfigured before them.

(Jesus extends his arms. Peter, James, and John fall to the ground and shade their eyes.)

Narrator   The face of Jesus shone like the sun, and his clothes became white as light. Moses and Elijah appeared.

(Moses and Elijah enter and go to Jesus, one on each side.)

Narrator   Moses and Elijah talked to Jesus. They spoke about the passion and death he would undergo in Jerusalem.

Peter   Lord, it is good that we are here. If you wish, I will make three tents here, one for you, one for Moses, and one for Elijah.

Narrator   While Peter was still speaking, a bright cloud cast a shadow over them. From the cloud came a voice.

Voice   This is my beloved Son, with whom I am will pleased. Listen to him.

(Peter, James, and John fall to the ground face down and tremble. Jesus walks over to them and touches each one.)

Jesus   Rise, and do not be afraid.

(Peter, James, and John sit up, open their eyes, and rub them. They look around.)

Narrator   They saw no one else, but Jesus alone.

Martha and Mary

Luke 10:38-42

(Martha stands in the center of the stage in front of chairs. Mary is in the background. Pot is on the floor, and dishes are on the table. Jesus and Disciples enter.)

Jesus   Martha! How are you?

Martha   *(excitedly)* Jesus! I'm fine. Welcome to Bethany. Supper is almost ready. Won't you join us?

Jesus   I'd love to.

Martha   Come in.

Mary   *(going to Jesus)* Master, it's so good to see you!

(Jesus and Disciples are seated. Mary sits at Jesus' feet. Martha goes to table and stirs the pot.)

Mary   What have you been doing, Jesus?

Jesus   We've been teaching in towns as we journey to Jerusalem.

(Martha sets table.)

Mary   Tell me. What did you teach at the last town you were in?

Jesus   Well, someone asked me what to do to have eternal life . . .

(Martha walks over to Jesus.)

Martha   *(hands on her hips)* Lord, do you not care that my sister has left me by myself to do the serving? Tell her to help me.

Jesus   *(shaking head)* Martha, Martha, you are anxious and worried about many things. There is need of only one thing. Mary has chosen the better part and it will not be taken from her.

Paying Taxes to Caesar

Matthew 22:15-22   Mark 12:13-17   Luke 20:20-26

(Pharisees enter. Pharisees' Disciples follow at a distance.)

Pharisee 1   *(to Pharisee 2)*   We must trap him in his speech.

Pharisee 2   Yes. If we make him look like a fool, his followers will leave him.

Pharisee 1   If we can get him to speak against the government, we might be rid of him.

Pharisee 2   I've got it. *(to Pharisees' Disciples)* Come here.

(Pharisees' Disciples walk up to Pharisees 1, 2.)

Pharisee 2   Find Jesus. Ask him if it is lawful to pay tax to Caesar. *(Laughs wickedly.)* That'll stump him.

(Pharisees 1, 2 exit laughing. Jesus and Crowd enter. Pharisees' Disciples walk over to Jesus.)

Pharisees' Disciple 1   Ah, Teacher, we know that you are a truthful man and that you teach the way of God in accordance with the truth.

Pharisees' Disciple 2   And you are not concerned with anyone's opinion, for you do not regard a person's status.

Pharisees' Disciple 1   Tell us, then, what is your opinion: Is it lawful to pay the census tax to Caesar or not?

Pharisees' Disciple 2   Should we pay or should we not pay?

(Jesus gives them a hard look.)

Jesus   Why are you testing me, you hypocrites? Show me the coin that pays the census tax.

(Pharisees' Disciple 1 opens his money bag and takes out a coin.)

Pharisees'
Disciple 1   *(handing the coin to Jesus)*   Here. A Roman coin.

    Jesus   *(holding up coin)*   Whose image is this and whose inscription?

Pharisees'
Disciple 1, 2   Caesar's.

    Jesus   *(calmly)*   Then repay to Caesar what belongs to Caesar and to God what belongs to God.

(Pharisees' Disciples 1, 2 gasp. They turn and walk away quickly.)

The Woman Caught in Adultery
John 8:2-11

Narrator   Early one morning Jesus walked into the temple area.

(Jesus enters. Crowd enters gradually. Jesus sits.)

Jesus   I am the light of the world. Whoever follows me will not walk in darkness . . .

Narrator   Jesus was interrupted when some scribes and Pharisees brought a woman to him. She had been caught in adultery.

(Scribes and Pharisees enter with Woman. Pharisee 1 and Pharisee 2 are on either side of her.)

Pharisee 1   *(pointing to ground before Jesus, to Woman)* Stand there in the middle.

(Woman stands before Jesus with her head down.)

Pharisee 2   Teacher, this woman was caught in the very act of committing adultery.

Scribe 1   Now in the law, Moses commanded us to stone such women.

Scribe 2   So what do you say?

Narrator   They said this to test him, so that they could have some charge to bring against him.

(Jesus bends down and writes with his finger on the ground.)

Pharisee 1   Well, Jesus, what do you say?

Pharisee 2   Do we stone her or not?

(Jesus straightens up.)

Jesus   Let the one among you who is without sin be the first to throw a stone at her.

(Jesus bends down and writes on the ground. Scribes and Pharisees watch him write. One by one they leave. When Jesus and Woman are alone, Jesus straightens up.)

Jesus   Woman, where are they? Has no one condemned you?

Woman   No one, sir.

Jesus   Neither do I condemn you. Go, and from now on do not sin anymore.

(Woman walks away slowly, looking back at Jesus from time to time.)

HAS NO ONE CONDEMNED YOU JN8·10

Zacchaeus, the Tax Collector
Luke 19:1-10

(Crowd and Person are on one side of stage facing the wings. Tree is on the other side. Zacchaeus stands between the Crowd and the tree.)

Narrator   Once Jesus came to Jericho, intending to pass right through the town. Now a man there named Zacchaeus was a chief tax collector and a wealthy man. He was not liked because of his job. He wanted to see who Jesus was, but he could not see him because of the crowd. He was short.

(Crowd looks off stage. Zacchaeus tries to look between people.)

Person 1   I see him. I see him. He's coming.

(Zacchaeus jumps up and down to see. He shakes his head and looks frustrated. He sees the tree, his face brightens, and he snaps his fingers. He runs to the tree and climbs up.)

Narrator   From the sycamore tree Zacchaeus had a good view of Jesus.

(Jesus enters and Crowd moves along with him towards the tree. At the tree Jesus looks up.)

Jesus   *(shouting)* Zacchaeus, come down quickly, for today I must stay at your house.

(Zacchaeus climbs down.)

Zacchaeus   You don't mean it! How wonderful. I am honored. Come with me.

(Jesus and Zacchaeus begin to walk off.)

Person 2   *(angrily)* He has gone to stay at the house of a sinner.

(Zacchaeus stops.)

Zacchaeus   *(to Jesus)* Behold, half of my possessions, Lord, I shall give

ZACCHÆUS, HURRY DOWN · LK 19 · 5

to the poor, and if I have stolen anything from anyone I shall repay it four times over.

Jesus   (to Zacchaeus)   Today salvation has come to this house because this man too is a descendant of Abraham. For the Son of Man has come to seek and to save what is lost.

(Jesus and Zacchaeus walk off.)

The Widow's Offering

Mark 12:41-44   Luke 21:1-4

(Chair is opposite bowl. Jesus and Disciples 1, 2 enter. Jesus walks away and sits down.)

Narrator   One day Jesus sat watching people put money into the temple treasury.

(Wealthy Person 1 enters, empties bag into bowl, and exits. Wealthy Person 2 enters, empties bag into bowl, and exits.)

Disciple 1   *(to Disciple 2)*   Wow! Did you see that?

Narrator   A poor widow came along with a few cents.

(Widow enters and shyly puts two small coins in bowl. She exits.)

Jesus   *(to Disciples)*   Come here.

(Disciples go to Jesus.)

Jesus   Amen, I say to you, this poor widow put in more than all the other contributors to the treasury. For they have all contributed from their surplus wealth, but she, from her poverty, has offered all she had.

The Entry into Jerusalem

Matthew 21:1-11 Mark 11:1-11 Luke 19:28-40 John 12:12-19

(Jesus and Disciples enter. Bystander and colt are off to the side.)

Narrator   Jesus and his disciples walked toward Jerusalem.

Jesus   *(to Disciples 1, 2)*   The two of you go into the village opposite you. As you enter it you will find a colt on which no one has ever sat. Untie it and bring it here. And if anyone should ask you, "Why are you untying it?" you will answer, "The master has need of it."

(Disciples 1, 2 walk toward colt. Jesus and other Disciples sit down.)

Disciple 1   There's the colt, just as Jesus said.

(Disciple 2 unties the colt.)

HOSANNA MK 11·9

Bystander   What are you doing? Untying the colt?

Disciple 2   The master has need of it.

Bystander   Oh. O.K. then.

             (Disciples 1, 2 and Bystander go to Jesus. Disciple 2 leads colt.)

Disciple 1   *(to Jesus)* We found it.

             (Disciples throw cloaks over the colt. They help Jesus mount the colt. Crowd enters. Some throw cloaks on the ground. Others spread branches. Half the Crowd goes before Jesus and half follows him. He rides the colt.)

Disciples
and Crowd   Hosanna! Blessed is he who comes in the name of the Lord! Hosanna in the highest!

Pharisee 1   *(to Jesus)*   Teacher, stop them!

Jesus   I tell you, if they keep silent, the stones will cry out!

Narrator   The procession entered Jerusalem.

             (Person enters.)

Person   Who is this?

Crowd   This is Jesus the prophet, from Nazareth in Galilee.

Pharisee 2   *(to Pharisee 1)* Look, the whole world is running after him!

The Last Supper

Matthew 26:20-30   Mark 14:17-26   Luke 22:14-22   John 13:1-27

(Jesus and Twelve Apostles are eating around table. John is next to Jesus.)

Narrator   At Jesus' direction the apostles had prepared for the Passover meal in a large upper room in Jerusalem. When it was evening, he came there with the Twelve.

(Jesus stands, removes his robe, and ties a towel around his waist. He pours water into a basin. He goes to each Apostle and "washes" and "dries" their feet. Peter is last.)

Peter   Master, are you going to wash my feet?

Jesus   What I am doing, you do not understand now, but you will understand later.

Peter   You will never wash my feet.

Jesus   Unless I wash you, you will have no inheritance with me.

Peter   *(extending hands)*   Master, then not only my feet, but my hands and head as well.

(Jesus "washes" and "dries" Peter's feet. Then he puts on robe and goes to table.)

Jesus   Do you realize what I have done for you? You call me "teacher" and "master," and rightly so, for indeed I am. If I, therefore, the master and teacher, have washed your feet, you ought to wash one another's feet. Amen, amen, I say to you, one of you will betray me.

(Apostles look at one another.)

John   Surely it is not I, Lord?

Apostles   Surely it is not I, Lord?

Jesus   It is the one to whom I hand the bread after I have dipped it.

(Jesus dips bread in a bowl and hands it to Judas. All continue eating.)

Jesus   *(taking bread)*   Blessed are you, O Lord our God, King of the universe. You have made this bread holy. *(Breaks bread and passes it to Apostles)* Take and eat. This is my body. Do this in remembrance of me.
           (taking the cup) Blessed are you, O Lord our God, King of the universe, Creator of the vine.*(Gives cup to Apostles.)* Drink from it, all of you, for this is my blood of the covenant, which will be shed on behalf of many for the forgiveness of sins.

(All sing a psalm and exit.)

The Agony in the Garden

Matthew 26:36-56   Mark 14:32-52   Luke 22:39-53   John 18:1-12

Narrator   After supper on Thursday evening, Jesus and the disciples went to the Mount of Olives. They stopped at the garden of Gethsemane.

(Jesus and Eleven Apostles enter.)

Jesus   Sit here while I go over there and pray. Peter, James, and John, come with me.

(Apostles sit. Jesus, Peter, James, and John walk over to side.)

Jesus   My soul is sorrowful even to death. Remain here and keep watch with me.

(Peter, James, and John sit. Jesus goes forward a little and falls to the ground, praying. Peter, James, and John sleep.)

Jesus   My Father, if it is possible, let this cup pass from me. Yet, not as I will but as you will.

(Jesus rises and goes to Peter, James, and John.)

Jesus   *(to Peter)*   So you could not keep watch with me for one hour? Watch and pray that you may not undergo the test. The spirit is willing, but the flesh is weak.

(Jesus goes forward, kneels, and prays. Peter, James, and John sleep.)

Jesus   My Father, if it is not possible that this cup pass without my drinking it, your will be done.

(Jesus rises and goes to Peter, James, and John. He looks at them and shakes his head. He goes forward, kneels, and prays.)

Jesus   My Father, if it is not possible that this cup pass without my drinking it, your will be done.

(Jesus rises and goes to Peter, James, and John.)

Jesus   Are you still sleeping and taking your rest? Behold the hour is at hand when the Son of Man is to be handed over to sinners. Get up, let us go. Look, my betrayer is at hand.

(Judas, Soldiers, and Malchus enter.)

Narrator   Judas had arranged with the soldiers that he would identify Jesus by kissing him.

Judas   *(kissing Jesus)* Hail, Rabbi!

Jesus   Friend, do what you have come for.

(Soldiers grab Jesus. Peter draws sword and swings at Malchus.)

Malchus   *(screaming)* Ahhhh! My ear.

(Jesus touches Malchus and heals ear.)

Malchus   *(amazed)* I'm healed!

Jesus   *(to Peter)* Put your sword back into its sheath. All who take the sword will perish by the sword. Do you think that I cannot call upon my Father and he will not provide me at this moment with more than twelve legions of angels?
    (to Soldiers) Have you come out as against a robber, with swords and clubs to seize me? Day after day I sat teaching in the temple area, yet you did not arrest me. But this is your hour, the time for the power of darkness.

(Apostles run away.)

The Trial Before Pilate

Mark 15:1-20   Matthew 27:11-31   Luke 23:1-25   John 18:28-19:16

(Pilate stands on one side of the stage with his back to the other. Soldiers stand in the background, arms crossed.)

Narrator   On the morning after Jesus was arrested, soldiers brought him from Caiaphas, the high priest, to Pilate, the Roman procurator.

(Jesus and Jewish Leaders enter from opposite side. They stop some distance from Pilate.)

Jewish
Leader 1   Pilate, we cannot enter your building or we will not be able to eat the Passover meal.

(Pilate walks over to Jewish Leaders.)

Pilate   What charge do you bring against this man?

Jewish
Leader 2   If he were not a criminal, we would not have handed him over to you.

Pilate   Take him yourselves and judge him according to your law.

Jewish
Leader 1   We do not have the right to execute anyone.

(Pilate returns to his side of the stage. He turns to face the Jewish Leaders.)

Pilate   *(beckoning to Jesus)* Come here.

(Jesus walks to Pilate.)

Pilate   Are you the king of the Jews?

Jesus   Do you say this on your own accord or have others told you about me?

Pilate	I am not a Jew, am I? Your own nation and the chief priests handed you over to me. What have you done?
Jesus	My kingdom does not belong to this world. If my kingdom did belong to this world, my attendants would be fighting to keep me from being handed over to the Jews. But as it is, my kingdom is not here.
Pilate	Then you are a king?
Jesus	You say I am a king. For this I was born and for this I came into the world, to testify to the truth. Everyone who belongs to the truth listens to my voice.
Pilate	What is truth?

(Pilate goes to Jewish Leaders.)

Pilate	I find no guilt in him. But you have a custom that I release one prisoner to you at Passover. Do you want me to release to you Barabbas or Jesus, called Messiah?

(Messenger enters and goes to Pilate.)

Messenger	Sir, your wife sends you a message. She says, "Have nothing to do with that righteous man. I have suffered much in a dream today because of him."
Pilate	*(to Jewish Leaders)* Which of the two do you wish me to release to you?
Jewish Leaders	Barabbas!
Pilate	*(to Soldiers)* Take him away and whip him.

(Soldiers and Jesus exit.)

Narrator	The soldiers whipped Jesus. They wove a crown of thorns and placed it on his head. They clothed him in a purple cloak and mocked him saying, "Hail, king of the Jews." Then they returned him to Pilate.

(Soldiers and Jesus enter. Pilate goes to Jewish Leaders.)

Pilate   Look, I am bringing him out to you, so that you may know that I find no guilt in him.

(Pilate motions for Jesus to come. The soldiers bring Jesus to Pilate. Pilate gestures toward Jesus.)

Pilate   Behold, the man!

Jewish
Leaders   Crucify him. Crucify him.

Pilate   Take him yourselves and crucify him. I find no guilt in him.

Jewish
Leaders   We have a law, and according to that law he ought to die, because he made himself the Son of God.

(Pilate puts his hand to his face in fear and returns to his side of stage.)

Pilate   *(to Jesus)* Where are you from? *(Long pause)* Do you not speak to me? Do you not know that I have power to crucify you?

Jesus   You would have no power over me if it had not been given to you from above. For this reason the one who handed me over to you has the greater sin.

(Pilate goes to Jewish Leaders.)

Pilate   This man should be released.

Jewish
Leaders   If you release him, you are not a friend of Caesar. Everyone who makes himself a king opposes Caesar.

(Pilate takes Jesus to chair and has him sit.)

Pilate   *(to Jewish Leaders)* Behold your king.

Jewish
Leaders   Take him away. Take him away. Crucify him.

Pilate   Shall I crucify your king?

Jewish
Leaders   We have no king but Caesar.

(Pilate goes to bowl and washes his hands.)

Pilate   I am innocent of this man's blood. Look to it yourselves.

Jewish
Leaders   His blood be upon us and upon our children.

Pilate   *(to Soldiers)* Take him out and crucify him.

(Soldiers go to Jesus and roughly pull him up. Soldiers and Jesus exit. Jewish Leaders cheer.)

The Resurrection

John 20:1-18

(Peter and John are at the far side of the stage. Mary enters from the other side.)

Narrator   On the first day of the week, Mary of Magdala came to the tomb early in the morning, while it was still dark, and saw the stone removed from the tomb.

(Mary gasps and puts hands to face in horror. She runs to Peter and John.)

Mary   They have taken the Lord from the tomb, and we don't know where they put him.

(Peter and John run to the tomb. John arrives first and peers in the tomb. He waits for Peter. Peter arrives.)

John   I can see the burial cloths.

Peter   *(stooping and going in tomb)* Look. The cloth that covered his head is rolled up in a separate place.

(John stoops and goes in tomb. Peter and John exit. Mary stands weeping. Angels 1, 2 enter and sit in the tomb.)

Angel 1   Woman, why are you weeping?

(Jesus enters behind Mary.)

Mary   They have taken my Lord, and I don't know where they laid him.

(Mary turns and sees Jesus.)

Narrator   Mary thought Jesus was the gardener.

Mary   *(to Jesus)* Sir, if you carried him away, tell me where you laid him, and I will take him.

Jesus   Mary!

Mary   (excitedly) Rabbouni! *(Kneels and clasps Jesus' knees.)*

Jesus   Stop holding on to me, for I have not yet ascended to the Father. Go to my brothers and tell them I am going to my Father and your Father, to my God and your God.

        (Mary rises and exits.)

Mary   *(shouting offstage)* I have seen the Lord!

The Appearance to the Women
Matthew 28:1-10   Mark 16:1-8 Luke 24:1-12

(Stone is before tomb. Guards stand by it.)

Narrator   Very early when the sun had risen, on the first day of the week Mary of Magdala and other women went to the tomb. They brought spices to anoint Jesus.

(Mary and Women enter and walk toward tomb.)

Woman 1   Who will roll back the stone for us from the entrance to the tomb?

(Women shake.)

Woman 2   What was that?

Mary   An earthquake.

(Angel enters and rolls back stone. Guards faint.)

Angel   *(to Women)*   Do not be afraid! I know that you are seeking Jesus the crucified. He is not here, for he has been raised just as he said. Come and see the place where he lay. Then go quickly and tell his disciples, "He has been raised from the dead, and he is going before you to Galilee. There you will see him." Behold, I have told you.

(Women peer into tomb. They begin to run. Jesus enters and meets them.)

Jesus   Good morning!

Woman 1   Jesus.

Woman 2   Master.

(Women kneel and bow to Jesus.)

Jesus   Do not be afraid. Go tell my brothers to go to Galilee, and there they will see me.

(Disciples enter. Women go to them.)

Woman 1   Jesus is alive.

Woman 2   He is risen.

Disciple 1   That's nonsense!

Woman 1   He spoke to us.

Disciple 2   You're out of your mind!

(Group stands arguing. Peter leaves group, goes to tomb, and peers in. He stands up amazed.)

Peter   The tomb is empty! How can this be?

The Appearance on the Emmaus Road
Luke 24:13-35

Narrator   On the day of the Resurrection two disciples were going to a village seven miles from Jerusalem called Emmaus.

(Cleopas and Disciple enter.)

Cleopas   I can't believe he's dead.

Disciple   According to those women, he's not.

(Jesus enters and joins the Disciples.)

Jesus   What are you discussing as you walk along?

(Disciples stop.)

Cleopas   *(sadly)*   Are you the only visitor to Jerusalem who does not know of the things that have taken place there in these days?

THEY KNOW HIM IN THE BREAKING OF BREAD☙LK24-35

Jesus	What sort of things?
Disciple	The things that happened to Jesus the Nazarene, who was a prophet mighty in deed and word before God and all the people, how our chief priests and rulers both handed him over to a sentence of death and crucified him.
Cleopas	But we were hoping that he would be the one to redeem Israel. Besides all this, it is now the third day since this took place.
Disciple	Some women from our group, however, have astounded us. They were at the tomb early in the morning and did not find his body. They came back and reported that they had indeed seen a vision of angels who announced that he was alive.
Cleopas	Then some of those with us went to the tomb and found things just as the women had described, but him they did not see.
Jesus	Oh, how foolish you are! How slow of heart to believe all that the prophets spoke! Was it not necessary that the Messiah should suffer these things and enter into his glory? The Scriptures tell you this. Let me explain, beginning with Moses and the prophets.
	(Jesus, Cleopas, and Disciple walk on, talking.)
Narrator	Jesus explained to them what referred to him in all the Scriptures until they approached the village.
	(Cleopas and Disciples stop. Jesus keeps walking.)
Cleopas	Stay with us.
Disciple	It is nearly evening and the day is almost over.
Jesus	All right. I will.
	(Jesus smiles and he, Cleopas, and Disciple go to table and sit.)
Jesus	*(taking bread)* Blessed are You, O Lord our God, King of the universe.

(Jesus breaks the bread and passes it to Cleopas and Disciple.)

Cleopas
and
Disciple *(in awe)* Jesus!

(Jesus disappears backstage or under the table.)

Cleopas He's gone!

Disciple Weren't our hearts burning within us while he spoke to us on the way and opened the Scriptures to us?

Cleopas *(excitedly)* Let's go back to Jerusalem and tell the others what happened.

(Cleopas and Disciple rise and run off.)

The Appearance to the Apostles
Luke 24:36-51

(Disciples are on stage, talking excitedly.)

Disciple 1
How amazing that he walked to Emmaus with those disciples.

Disciple 2
And they didn't know him until he broke bread!

(Jesus enters and stands in the middle of them.)

Jesus
Peace be with you.

(Disciples gasp and shrink back, frightened.)

Jesus
Why are you troubled? And why do questions arise in your hearts? Look at my hands and my feet, that it is I myself. Touch me and see, *(extending hands)* because a ghost does not have flesh and bones *(gesturing to feet)* as you can see I have.

(Disciples come forward with joy and amazement.)

Jesus
Have you anything here to eat?

(Disciple 1 takes fish from table and gives it to Jesus.)

Jesus
Thank you.

(Jesus "eats" the fish while the Disciples watch.)

Jesus
These are my words that I spoke to you while I was still with you, that everything written about me in the law of Moses and in the prophets and psalms must be fulfilled.

Thus it is written that the Messiah would suffer and rise from the dead on the third day and that repentance, for the forgiveness of sins, would be preached in his name to all the nations, beginning from Jerusalem. You are witnesses of these things.

And behold I am sending the promise of my Father upon you. But stay in the city until you are clothed with power from on high. Come with me.

(Jesus and Disciples exit.)

Narrator   Jesus led the disciples to Bethany, raised his hands and blessed them. As he blessed them he parted from them and was taken up to heaven.

PEACE TO YOU · LK 24·36

The Appearance to Thomas
John 20:19-29

(Disciples are on stage.)

Narrator   On the evening of the Resurrection, the first day of the week, the disciples were behind locked doors in fear of the Jews.

(Jesus enters and stands in the middle of the Disciples. They step back in fear.)

PUT YOUR HAND INTO MY SIDE JN 20:27

Jesus   Peace be with you. It is really I, Jesus. See. *(Extends his hands.)* And see. *(Points to his side.)*

Disciple 1   Jesus. I'm so happy.

Disciple 2   We thought you were dead.

(Disciples laugh. Clasp their hands together. Show joy.)

Jesus   Peace be with you. As the Father has sent me, so I send you.

(Breathes on the Disciples gently.) Receive the Holy Spirit. Whose sins you forgive are forgiven them, and whose sins you retain are retained.

(Jesus exits. Thomas enters.)

Disciple 2   Thomas! You missed it.

Disciple 3   We have seen the Lord.

Thomas   *(shaking head)* Unless I see the mark of the nails in his hands and put my finger into the nailmarks and put my hand into his side, I will not believe.

Narrator   A week later the disciples were again inside behind locked doors, and Thomas was with them.

(Jesus enters and stands among the Disciples.)

Jesus   Peace be with you. *(to Thomas)* Put your finger here *(extending hand)* and see my hands, and bring your hand and put it into my side, and do not be unbelieving, but believe.

Thomas   *(kneeling)* My Lord and my God!

Jesus   Have you come to believe because you have seen me? Blessed are those who have not seen and have believed.

DIRECTOR'S HANDBOOK

Tips for Putting on Playlets

1. Make a copy of the playlet for each participant who has a speaking part or a major role. Highlight, or have the students highlight, all of their parts, including stage directions.

2. Make an identification sign or headband for each character.

3. Allow as many students as possible to particpate in the playlet. Cast names marked + in the Director's Handbook can be adjusted to the size of your class.

4. Prepare the props that are suggested for some playlets. Printed signs indicating the setting are also helpful, particularly if the location changes during the play. Pictures of scenery drawn on the blackboard could serve as the backdrop for the playlet.

5. List the characters on the board so that students can sign for parts before class. They might have time to practice and even to memorize their lines.

6. Arrange to have actors rehearse together during class while the rest of the students are engaged in another activity. A teacher aide might take the group to another room for practice.

7. Encourage the participants
   to look up from their scripts as much as possible
   to speak so as to be heard and understood
   to avoid having their backs to the audience
   to use expression in interpreting their lines
   to be creative in adding movements and gestures.

8. Before the playlet begins, have the characters introduce themselves to the audience, especially if they are not wearing identification.

9. Compliment the group or individuals for a job well done.

10. Make sure that each student has a speaking role at some time, and is not always just a member of the crowd.

Caution: Avoid putting on a playlet only for the sake of putting on a playlet. With no proper introduction or follow-up, a playlet is a waste of time instead of meaningful educational experience.

THE ANNOUNCEMENT OF JOHN'S BIRTH

Luke 1:5-25

CAST
Narrator
Zechariah
Angel Gabriel
Persons 1, 2, 3+

PROPS
Table for altar
Incense

THEMES
Infancy narratives, John the Baptist, openness to God, faith

COMMENTS
Elizabeth and Zechariah were righteous people who were childless, like Abraham and Sarah. During prayer, God reveals startling news to Zechariah. Zechariah and Elizabeth will have a son who will be great in God's sight. The day John's birth was announced was special for Zechariah. Out of eight hundred priests in his division, he was chosen by lot to offer incense that day in the Holy Place of the Temple. The many people present suggest that he was carrying this office out during the evening hours. Gabriel appears and says "Do not be afraid" to Zechariah, just what he will say to Mary six months later. These words often preface a redemptive act of God. Gabriel's words to Zechariah follow the formula for a birth announcement commonly used in the Scriptures. The angel foretells that John will be a Nazarite dedicated to God, as Samson was. God will empower him to be the forerunner of Jesus and help bring about the messianic age. Like Elijah, he will announce the Lord. He will be a great prophet. Zechariah is left speechless by the good news—either because he lacked faith or because he was overcome by joy.

POINTS FOR DISCUSSION
• How this event compares with the announcement of Jesus' birth
• Trusting in God to do the impossible
• The nature and role of angels
• Being open to God in prayer

THE ANNUNCIATION

Luke 1:26-38
Fourth Sunday of Advent B

CAST
Narrator
Gabriel
Mary

THEMES
Infancy narratives, obedience, openness to God, Mary, identity of Jesus, the Spirit

COMMENTS
The announcement of the immediate coming of the Messiah was made to Mary, a virgin in Nazareth. Nazareth was an insignificant town scorned by Palestinians. Yet it would be the hometown of the Savior of the world. Mary would have a son conceived miraculously by the overshadowing of the Holy Spirit.

This conception surpasses the conception of John, whose parents conceived him naturally, although they were advanced in age.

The angel Gabriel greets Mary with words of great praise. He discloses that God has chosen her to bear a son who is the son of God. She is to name him Jesus, which means "God saves." The words Gabriel used to describe Mary's son, such as "Son of the Most High," are those that signify God's redeeming presence in the Hebrew Scriptures. Mary is espoused to Joseph, who is of the family of David. Because Joseph would be Jesus' legal father, it is through him, not Mary, that Jesus would trace his lineage.

Mary accepts God's will for her and merits her name, which in Hebrew means "exalted one." In trust and obedience she agrees to be a virgin-mother, the mother of the Savior. She stands as a model for all who are called to bring forth Christ into the world and to further his kingdom.

POINTS FOR DISCUSSION
- The wonder of God's becoming a human being like us to save us
- The honor it is for Mary to be Mother of God and to help save humankind
- Other privileges Mary has that flow from her role as Mother of God
- The miraculous conception of Jesus, and Mary's dilemma
- The nature and role of angels
- Mary's openness to the will of God and her complete faith
- Ways to show devotion to Mary, especially through imitation

THE VISITATION

Luke 1:39-56
Fourth Sunday of Advent C

CAST | PROPS
Narrator | Pot and ladle or broom
Mary | Two chairs
Elizabeth

THEMES
Infancy narratives, Mary, John the Baptist, service, the poor

COMMENTS
Mary's union with God prompts her to self-less action. Hastening to assist her elderly relative, Elizabeth, she undertakes a journey of about ninety miles. When the two women meet, Elizabeth recognizes the great blessing that has come to Mary. The baby in her womb leaps, a sign of messianic joy. It is Jesus who is the reason for John's greatness and John's mission in life. John is quickened with new life, the life of the Spirit. Tradition holds that at that moment John the Baptist was freed from sin.

Mary's hymn of praise is called the Magnificat, from the Latin for the opening words. It is similar to Hannah's song (1 Samuel 2:1-10). The church prays the Magnificat every day in evening prayer. In this canticle, after reflecting on her role as handmaid favored by God, Mary recalls the great themes of salvation history: God's surprising reversals as he acts on behalf of the poor and needy. The rich and powerful are brought low, while the poor and humble are raised. Mary closes her song by proclaiming that God has kept the promise made to Abraham. Israel, a servant, has been favored.

POINTS FOR DISCUSSION
- Mary's selflessness in responding to Elizabeth's need
- Sacrifices that the visit must have entailed for Mary
- The relationship of Jesus and John in salvation history
- Why the Magnificat fits the occasion
- How we can love and serve the members of our family

THE BIRTH OF JOHN

Luke 1:57-78

CAST | PROPS
Narrator | Paper
Zechariah | Pencil
Elizabeth | Doll or blanket for baby
Persons 1, 2, 3+ |

THEMES
Infancy narratives, John the Baptist

COMMENTS
John is not named after his father, as was the custom. He who is to be the messenger of God is named by God. When Zechariah affirms the name John, he regains the power of speech. Everyone is filled with wonder, and Zechariah praises God. The first part of his canticle is modeled on Jewish circumcision ceremonies. The second part links John to the Savior. It gives his identity in relation to Jesus. The hopes and promises of the Jewish forefathers will soon be fulfilled. The dayspring will dawn to save people from darkness. Zechariah's song is prayed every day in the morning praise of the Liturgy of the Hours, the official prayer of the church.

POINTS FOR DISCUSSION
• The obedience of Zechariah in naming his son John
• The role of John
• Reasons we have for blessing the Lord

THE BIRTH OF JESUS

Luke 2:1-20
Christmas Mass at Midnight A, B, C
Christmas Mass at Dawn A, B, C
January 1, Octave of Christmas, Solemnity
of Mary, Mother of God A, B, C

CAST | PROPS
Narrator | Doll or blanket for baby
Mary | Box for manger
Joseph | Shepherds' staffs
Innkeeper | Scroll for innkeeper
Angel 1 | Cloths for swaddling
Angels+ | clothes in basket or bag
Shepherds 1, 2+ | Two chairs

THEMES
Infancy narratives, identity of Jesus, Mary, the good news, obedience to law, poverty

COMMENTS
In the Scriptures, the birth of the Savior is told in the context of the Roman empire. Mary and Joseph are good citizens responding to a call for a worldwide census. People must return to their own towns to register. Because Joseph is of the House of David, he must return to Bethlehem, about ninety miles from Nazareth. Joseph finds shelter and privacy in a room where people kept livestock. The stable was probably a cave, the back room of a house. There Mary gives birth to Jesus. She wraps him in swaddling clothes, long strips that Palestinians used so that their children would grow straight and strong. The newborn boy, who would someday be the bread of life, is placed in a manger, a feeding trough. He is Mary's firstborn, the first of many others—his future followers.

Angels announce to shepherds the good news of the child's birth. Shepherds are poor people whose job was that of the patriarchs: to guard and guide. In their proclamation, the angels call Jesus Savior, Messiah, and Lord. The news is especially exciting for the shepherds because the Messiah has appeared in humble surroundings, like one of them.

POINTS FOR DISCUSSION
- The obedience of Mary and Joseph to civil law
- The poverty God chose to be born in
- The love of God the Father in sending the gift of his Son
- Why the news of the angels is good news
- The significance of the shepherds
- Ways Jesus comes to us today
- How to make room for God in our lives

THE VISIT OF THE MAGI

Matthew 2:1-12
Epiphany A, B, C

CAST	PROPS
Narrator	Star
Magi 1, 2, 3	Chair
Herod	Doll or blanket for
Priests 1, 2+	infant
Scribes 1, 2+	Three gifts to represent
Mary	gold, frankincense, and
	myrrh

THEMES
Infancy narratives, the good news, identity of Jesus, Gentiles

COMMENTS
The story of the Magi confirms that Jesus is the king, the Messiah who would be born in David's city. Magi was a term for people skilled in supernatural knowledge and power. The gospel's Magi from the East were probably from Mesopotamia, the home of astrology. A popular belief was that a new star appeared whenever a person was born. When the star appears, the Magi go to the Jewish people to find out about the Messiah. The Jewish prophets tell them that the king is to be born in Bethlehem. Only after the Magi are in Jerusalem does the star guide them to the house where Jesus is.

In Matthew's gospel, it is the Gentiles, not the shepherds, who first worship Jesus. The Magi prostrate themselves before him. The three presents they bring have led to the belief that there were three Magi. Tradition has even named them Caspar, Melchior, and Balthasar. Their gifts are interpreted as symbols of the child. There is gold, for a king; frankincense, for a god; and myrrh, a sweet-smelling resin used in anointing for burial, to signify his death.

The conflict between Jesus and official Judaism is already present in the infancy narratives as Herod makes plans to murder the new king of the Jews.

The feast of Epiphany (manifestation of God), January 6, is called Little Christmas. Some people exchange gifts on this day. Priests may give an Epiphany house blessing, in which they write a code like 19 + C + M + B + 90 above the door. The letters represent the Magi; the numbers, the year; and the crosses, like compass points, all nations.

POINTS FOR DISCUSSION
- The little that is known of the astrologers from the East and the legends that have arisen about them
- The hint of the conflict and suffering that Jesus will face
- The significance of the fact that the Magi were Gentiles who came to honor Jesus
- The kind of king Jesus is
- What gifts we might give to God
- The similarity of the Holy Innocents and the babies killed in abortion

- How people celebrate Epiphany (in Puerto Rico, for example, children receive gifts on this day)

THE PRESENTATION

Luke 2:22-38
Sunday in the Octave of Christmas B

CAST | PROPS
Narrator | Doll or blanket for baby
Mary | Two birds in a cage
Joseph |
Simeon |
Anna |

THEMES

Infancy narratives, Mary, obedience to law, poverty, identity of Jesus, faithfulness, the suffering of Jesus

COMMENTS

Mary and Joseph take Jesus to Jerusalem for his presentation. In this ceremony, the firstborn son is consecrated to the Lord. Actually, Jesus has always belonged to the Father, but Mary and Joseph fulfill the Jewish Law. Mary and Joseph offer not a lamb, but the offering of the poor: a pair of turtle-doves. Simeon, a devout man who had difficult days of service in the Temple, was inspired by the Spirit to come to the Temple when Jesus was there. The Spirit had revealed to him that he would not die until he had seen the Savior. As all rabbis did when blessing children, Simeon takes Jesus into his arms and blesses God. His canticle declares universal salvation. In blessing the parents, Simeon predicts the child's destiny and foretells that Mary will be linked with Jesus in his redemptive suffering. The church, too, experiences his suffering and sorrow. Simeon, symbol of old Israel, having

witnessed the fulfillment of God's promises, can depart in peace.

Anna, a holy widow and one of Israel's faithful people, recognizes the Messiah and thanks God. She proclaimed the good news to all who waited for salvation.

POINTS FOR DISCUSSION
- What the poverty of Mary and Joseph teaches
- How God rewarded the faithfulness of Simeon and Anna
- The seven sorrows of Mary
- Rules and customs of our religion that we should follow

THE BOY JESUS IN THE TEMPLE

Luke 2:41-52
Sunday in the Octave of Christmas C

CAST | PROPS
Narrator | Chairs for Jesus and
Jesus | Teachers
Mary |
Joseph |
Relatives 1, 2+ |
John |
Teachers 1, 2+ |

THEMES

Infancy narratives, identity of Jesus, obedience, Mary, ministry

COMMENTS

Jewish people were obliged to travel to Jerusalem for three major feasts: Passover, Pentecost, and Tabernacles. Passover was celebrated for eight days. Mary, Joseph, and Jesus go to Jerusalem for Passover when Jesus is twelve years old, a year before he officially reaches manhood. This visit foreshadows Jesus' going to Jerusalem for

Passover at the end of his life. On the way home, Mary and Joseph discover that Jesus is missing. They search for him for three days—a time symbolic of the resurrection. Mary and Joseph find their son in the Temple, talking to the teachers. He explains to them that he is about his mission: his Father's work. Here he is not referring to his father Joseph, but is calling God his Father for the first time. The gospel says that Mary and Joseph do not understand what Jesus meant. Mary must have thought with sorrow of her future separation from him. She ponders the mystery she is sharing in.

Jesus returns to Nazareth with his parents. There, under their guidance, he grows in all ways to perfect manhood.

POINTS FOR DISCUSSION
- How Mary and Joseph must have felt while Jesus was missing
- Why Jesus stayed behind and what it signified
- Mary's private pondering of the actions of Jesus
- Examples of how Jesus probably was obedient to Mary and Joseph
- How children today can show obedience in imitation of Jesus

THE BAPTISM OF JESUS

Matthew 3:4-17   Mark 1:4-11
Luke 3: 7-22   John 1:19-34
Sunday after January 6 A, B, C

CAST	PROP
Narrator	Large seashell
John	
Jesus	
Priest	
Person	
Crowd+	
Voice	

THEMES
Identity of Jesus, John the Baptist, humility, conversion, mission of Jesus, the Spirit

COMMENTS
John carries on the role of Isaiah and Elijah. The greatest prophet, he prepares people for the Messiah. He preaches conversion and repentance, a complete internal turning of the heart toward God. His baptism is a sign of this repentance. John claims that the one to come is mightier than he in the war against evil. He is not worthy even to be his slave and untie his sandals. When Jesus asks for baptism, John recognizes him.

Although Jesus has no need of repentance, and therefore no need of baptism, he acts as humanity's representative. At his baptism, the Holy Spirit, who overshadowed Mary at his conception, overshadows him to begin his mission. On Pentecost, the Spirit will come to the church and anoint the followers of Jesus for mission. Jesus goes down into the water. When he comes up, God declares him "my beloved Son." In Christian baptism we, too, are claimed as sons and daughters of God. But, unlike John's baptism, our baptism actually gives us the gift of the Spirit.

- The importance of repentance for salvation
- What baptism is a sign of
- The significance of Jesus' baptism
- The difference between John's baptism and the sacrament of baptism
- Signs that a person is really converted
- What John the Baptist might say to us today

THE TEMPTATION OF JESUS

Matthew 4:1-11   Mark 1:12-13
Luke 4:1-13
First Sunday of Lent A, B, C

CAST	PROPS
Narrator	Rocks
Jesus	Two chairs for Temple
Devil	and mountain
Angels 1, 2+	

THEMES
Temptation, identity of Jesus, mission of Jesus

COMMENTS
The temptation story shows the humanity of Jesus. It also depicts Christ's overthrow of Satan's empire. Jesus goes to the desert, the place where evil spirits dwell according to tradition. He is there for forty days, which parallels the forty-year sojourn of the Israelites in the desert. The temptations are given in different orders in Matthew and Luke, but the scriptural answers to each are the same. The temptations test Jesus as Messiah. He is tempted to be a messiah of pleasure (turning stones to bread), a messiah of power (owning nations), and a messiah of fantastic feats (surviving a leap from the Temple parapet). Victoriously, Jesus rejects these temptations and embraces the role of true Messiah, the suffering servant. He will one day call Peter Satan when Peter tries to dissuade him from the path of the cross.

The outcome of the battle in the desert is demonstrated later in the exorcisms Jesus performs. As the church faces temptations, it looks to Christ's example as he deals with temptations against his mission.

POINTS FOR DISCUSSION
- The reality of Satan, who he is, and how he operates
- The steps of temptation
- Helps we have to resist temptation
- What temptations are the greatest for people today, for students today

THE FIRST APOSTLES

John 1:35-51
Second Sunday of the Year B

CAST	PROPS
Narrator	Table
Jesus	Three chairs
John	Tree, or drawing of tree
Disciple	on board
Andrew	
Simon Peter	
Philip	
Nathanael	

THEMES
Discipleship, identity of Jesus, Peter

COMMENTS
The first disciples of Jesus originally were John's disciples. They accept Jesus and call him Rabbi, the title of a teacher. Andrew and the other disciple (perhaps John) respond to Christ's invitation "Come and see." So memorable is this event that even the

hour is included in the gospel. The two disciples probably spend the night with Jesus. The next day, when Andrew brings his brother Peter to meet Jesus, Jesus changes his name to Cephas. This name change signifies that Simon is assuming a new way of life.

Nathanael is commonly identified with Bartholomew. When Jesus refers to some personal incident in Nathanael's life ("I saw you under the fig tree"), Nathanael acknowledges him as Son of God and King of Israel. The angels ascending and descending on the Son of Man is a reference to Jacob's ladder. In a vision, the patriarch Jacob saw a ladder, a mediator between God and man. The "far greater things" that Nathanael will see is the glory of God manifested in Jesus, our divine mediator.

POINTS FOR DISCUSSION
- The attraction of Jesus
- The symbolism of a name change
- The strengths and weaknesses of the apostles
- Why the students choose to follow Jesus
- What it means to be a follower of Jesus

THE CALL OF THE FIRST APOSTLES

Matthew 4:18-22   Mark 1:16-20
Third Sunday of the Year B

CAST	PROPS
Narrator	Rows of chairs for two
Jesus	boats
Peter	Nets
Andrew	
James	
John	
Zebedee	
Hired Men 1, 2+	

THEMES
Discipleship, ministry

COMMENTS
The three disciples who form the inner circle (Peter, James, and John) appear in the account of the call of the first disciples. As Jesus passes by, he calls them and Andrew to follow him. His call and their response are direct and immediate. The fishermen drop everything to come after him. Jesus' power over them motivates them to leave their jobs and their homes to follow him. Discipleship can demand renunciation of possessions and family ties. Jesus promises to make these disciples fishers of men, a hint of their apostolic authority.

POINTS FOR DISCUSSION
- The qualities of the apostles' response to Jesus
- The role of the apostles in the church
- How Jesus calls people today
- What it most costs us to follow Jesus
- Vocations to the priesthood and religious life

THE CALL OF MATTHEW

Matthew 9:9:13   Mark 2:14-17
Luke 5:27-32
Tenth Sunday of the Year   A

CAST	PROPS
Narrator	Two or more tables
Jesus	
Matthew	
Sinners 1, 2+	
Disciples 1, 2+	
Pharisees 1, 2+	

THEMES
Discipleship, conversion, mission of Jesus

78

COMMENTS

Jesus calls Matthew to follow him, and Matthew leaves his tax collector's booth as promptly as the fishermen left their nets. As a tax collector, Matthew was considered a traitor, a sinner. He collected taxes from his own people for the oppressor Rome. By choosing Matthew to follow him, and by accepting his dinner invitation, Jesus underlines the fact that he came for sinners. The upright Jewish person did not associate or eat with sinners and Gentiles. But Jesus calls everyone to the messianic banquet. We all must admit we are sinners before we can go to him.

POINTS FOR DISCUSSION
* The reputation of tax collectors
* Possible reasons why Matthew responded so promptly
* Jesus' unconventional points of view and actions
* What our attitudes toward sinners should be

THE BLESSING OF THE CHILDREN

Matthew 19:13-15   Mark 10:13-16
Luke 18:15-17
Twenty-Seventh Sunday of the Year B

CAST
Jesus
Disciples 1, 2+
Mothers 1, 2, 3+
Child 1
Children+

PROPS
Chair
Dolls or blankets for babies

THEMES
Holiness, the kingdom, the poor

COMMENTS

Parents bring their children to Jesus for his blessing, and the disciples scold them. Jesus rebukes his disciples for turning the parents away. Then he embraces the children and blesses them. Children are little ones who had no rights or status in the ancient world. Jesus uses them as the model for his disciples. His followers are to be simple and small, not self-important. They are to be dependent on the Father and open to accepting the gift of the kingdom.

POINTS FOR DISCUSSION
* The meaning of a blessing
* Characteristics of children
* What this episode reveals about Jesus
* How we must be and act if we wish to enter the kingdom

THE CLEANSING OF THE TEMPLE

Mark 11:15-18   Matthew 21:12-13
Luke 19:45-46 John 2:13-22
Third Sunday of Lent B

CAST
Narrator
Jesus
Disciples 1, 2+
Moneychangers 1, 2+
Sellers of Doves 1, 2+
Jewish Persons 1, 2+
Oxen and Sheep+

PROPS
Twine for cords
Bags of coins
Bird cages
Tables
Chairs

THEMES
Prayer, the resurrection, identity of Jesus

COMMENTS
This event happened at Passover when there were great crowds in Jerusalem. Animals needed for sacrifice were sold at the Temple. Moneychangers were there because Greek

and Roman coins, which bore images, could not be used at the Temple. The whip Jesus used to clear the Temple was probably a symbol of authority, rather than for practical use. In John's gospel, Jesus attacks the institutions, whereas in Mark, he attacks the dishonesty of the the dealers.

Jesus refers to God here as "my Father." He calls the Temple a house of prayer for all nations, an indication of the universality of God's love and salvation. His cleansing is a symbolic action. It implies that the temple cult no longer has meaning. Prayer and faith are what matters. The temple that Jesus predicts will be raised up after three days is himself. He is the new temple that replaces the Temple. God is found in him.

POINTS FOR DISCUSSION
• Why Jesus drove the people out of the Temple
• What the event reveals about who Jesus is
• The meaning of just anger
• Our duty to correct abuses and unfair practices
• The customs and etiquette that show reverence in our churches

THE RICH YOUNG MAN

Mark 10:17-31 Matthew 19:16-26
Luke 18:18-27
Twenty-Eighth Sunday of the Year B

CAST
Jesus
Rich Man
Disciples 1, 2+

THEMES
Discipleship, holiness, riches, the kingdom

COMMENTS
Jesus points to keeping the law as the way to enter the kingdom. In addition, in Mark's gospel Jesus demands that his followers give away their possessions to be saved. In Matthew, such extreme renunciation is not a mandate but a counsel of perfection. In either case, Jesus reverses the Jewish concept that wealth is a sign of God's favor. It is a radical following of Jesus that is the way of salvation. We must find our security in him, and not in possessions. The motivation behind giving up possessions is not because they are evil, or that asceticism has value, but that we must show concern for the poor. The rich will have a difficult time doing this, but God can assist them. For the rich young man, it is too difficult. He is the only person in the gospels who refuses to follow Jesus. He does not respond to Jesus' love. His riches possess him.

POINTS FOR DISCUSSION
• What prevents the young man from following Jesus
• How Jesus feels
• Ways we can be prevented from following Jesus
• Signs of materialism in our age
• Our responsibility to help the poor

THE WITHERED FIG TREE

||||||||||||||||||||||||||||||||||||||||||||||||||||||||||||||||||||||||||||

Mark 11:12-14; 20-25   Matthew 21:18-22

CAST   *PROPS*
Narrator   Fig tree
Jesus   Withered fig tree
Peter
Disciples 1, 2+

THEMES
Prayer, faith, holiness

COMMENTS
The tree might symbolize Israel, or the end of the Temple and its worship. The tree is barren when Jesus is in need of it. Mark notes it was not the time for figs. The purpose of the tree is to bear fruit. This story recalls the parable of the Barren Fig Tree, in which the owner threatens to cast his barren tree into the fire. Jesus' action leads into a discussion of faith and prayer.

POINTS FOR DISCUSSION
• The mysteriousness of Jesus' action
• What good fruit Jesus looks to us to bear
• The characteristics and importance of prayer

THE SAMARITAN WOMAN

||||||||||||||||||||||||||||||||||||||||||||||||||||||||||||||||||||||||||||||||||

John 4:4-42
Third Sunday of Lent A

CAST   *PROPS*
Narrator   Pail
Jesus   Package, for food
Disciples 1, 2+   Chair
Woman
Samaritans 1, 2+

THEMES
Identity of Jesus, mission of Jesus, women, evangelization

COMMENTS
Jesus' conversation with the Samaritan woman was unconventional on two counts. First, she was a woman, and Jewish men didn't speak to women in public. Second, she was a Samaritan. The Samaritans were enemies of the Jewish people mostly because they had intermarried with their neighbors during the Exile and because they worshiped in their own temple instead of in Jerusalem. Usually, the Jewish people avoided passing through their territory, which lay between Judea and Galilee. It was surprising, too, that Jesus asked the woman for water since, according to Jewish law, Samaritan utensils for eating and drinking were ritually unclean.

Jesus offers the woman living water, the gift that confers eternal life (Christian baptism). As they converse, she constantly misinterprets his messages but comes to recognize him as prophet and eventually Messiah. He affirms that he is the Messiah by stating "I am he." The "I am" indicates divinity. It recalls the name Yahweh revealed to Moses, "I am who am." The Samaritan woman spreads the news about Jesus to her neighbors. They learn for themselves that Jesus is the Savior of the world.

POINTS FOR DISCUSSION
• Who the Samaritans were
• The woman's background
• The unusualness of Jesus' actions
• The meaning of living water
• The process by which the woman comes to faith
• How the neighbors come to believe in Jesus
• Who Jesus was
• Ways we can come to know Jesus better and evangelize others

81

THE PARDON OF THE SINFUL WOMAN

Luke 7:36-50
Eleventh Sunday of the Year   C

CAST	PROPS
Narrator	Table and four chairs
Jesus	Plates
Simon	Flask for ointment
Persons 1, 2+	
Woman	

THEMES

Forgiveness, mission of Jesus, conversion, love, women, sinners, hypocrisy

COMMENTS

The story of the Pardon of the Sinful Woman in Luke's gospel is very similar to the story of the Anointing at Bethany in the other gospels. The main difference is that the woman in Luke's story is a sinner.

Jesus is dining at the home of Simon, a Pharisee. A woman who is known to be a sinner comes to anoint Jesus' feet. She bursts into tears, then dries his feet with her hair.

Simon thinks to himself that Jesus is no prophet or he would not let the woman touch him. Then Jesus shows himself a prophet by reading Simon's mind. He explains that the woman has been forgiven, and she has shown more love than Simon himself. He tells a parable that illustrates how a person who has been forgiven more, loves more. Jesus forgives the woman and gives her peace.

POINTS FOR DISCUSSION

- The courage and love of the woman contrasted with Simon's behavior
- How the emotions of the woman must have changed during the event
- The meaning of conversion
- The purpose of the sacrament of reconciliation and its parts
- How we show love for Jesus

THE ANOINTING AT BETHANY

Matthew 26:6-13   Mark 14:3-9
John 12:1-8
Passion Sunday B

CAST	PROPS
Narrator	Table and chairs
Jesus	Jar
Simon	
Persons 1, 2+	
Woman	

THEMES

Love for Jesus, death of Jesus

COMMENTS

The details of this event differ from gospel to gospel. In Matthew and Mark, Jesus' head is anointed. It was the custom to anoint the heads of guests. In John, Jesus' feet are anointed. Matthew and Mark identify the host as Simon the leper. John identifies the woman as Mary, the sister of Lazarus, and Judas as the disciple who complains.

The perfume the woman uses is valued at three hundred days' wages. It was sealed in an alabaster vase, which was sealed in such a way that it kept the fragrance in and had to be broken to be used. Jesus shows appreciation for the woman's generous gesture and defends it. He states that it will always be remembered (and it has been so far). Jesus asserts that he will not always be there, whereas the poor will. And he describes the anointing as a preparation for his burial. Jesus never was anointed. His burial was hurried, and when the women did come to anoint him, he was already risen.

POINTS FOR DISCUSSION

- The extravagance of the woman's gesture
- Means we have to honor and glorify Jesus
- Actions of Christians today that others consider foolish

PETER'S PROFESSION OF FAITH

||||||||||||||||||||||||||||||||||||||||||||||||||||||||||||||||||||||

Matthew 16:13-20   Mark 8:27-30
Luke 9:18-21
Twelfth Sunday of the Year C
Twenty-First Sunday of the Year A
Twenty-Fourth Sunday of the Year B

CAST
Jesus
Peter
Disciples 1, 2, 3+

THEMES
Faith, identity of Jesus, Peter, the church

COMMENTS
Although the account begins with what people think of Jesus, the focus is what the apostles think of him. While others say he is a prophet returned to earth, Peter proclaims that Jesus is the Messiah, the fulfillment of the promises in the Hebrew Scriptures. Peter is the first person to do so. In response, Jesus declares that his church will be founded on Peter, whose name means rock. Death shall not overcome it.

Jesus' warning not to tell others is interpreted in different ways. It could be that he did not want people to follow him as the kind of Messiah they expected.

POINTS FOR DISCUSSION
• What we believe about Jesus
• Who Jesus is for you
• The special role of Peter and the popes in the church
• How the present pope guides the church

THE TRANSFIGURATION OF JESUS

||||||||||||||||||||||||||||||||||||||||||||||||||||||||||||||||||||||

Matthew 17:1-8   Mark 9:2-8
Luke 9:28-36
Second Sunday of Lent A, B, C

CAST   *PROP*
Narrator   Cloud
Jesus
Peter
James
John
Moses
Elijah
Voice

THEMES
Identity of Jesus, the resurrection, the suffering of Jesus

COMMENTS
At the Transfiguration, Jesus is revealed in glory to Peter, James, and John. It anticipates the resurrection glory of Jesus and confirms his Messiahship. The account is rooted in some mystical experience the three disciples had. They did not perceive the impact of it until after the resurrection. The event is linked by the expression "six days" to Peter's confession of faith at Caesarea Philippi.

Details of the story that are reminiscent of God's theophany on Sinai point to Jesus as the New Moses: the high mountain, the cloud, Moses' presence, and the tents. The apostles represent the new people of God. Moses and Elijah, who are present at the event, stand for the Law and the prophets. As such, they witness to Jesus. They discuss his fate, that he is to suffer and die. The cloud and the mountain symbolize God's presence, and Jesus' dazzling appearance signifies the divine world. The apostles fall to the ground in fear. They do not understand. The words of the Father confirm Jesus' role as the Messiah and reveal his Sonship.

POINTS FOR DISCUSSION
• How the Transfiguration story parallels that of Moses at Mount Sinai
• The significance of the presence of Elijah and Moses
• Reasons for the Transfiguration
• The Christian attitudes toward suffering and death

MARTHA AND MARY
||||||||||||||||||||||||||||||||||||||||||||||||||||||||||||||||||||||||||||||

Luke 10:38-42
Sixteenth Sunday of the Year C

CAST
Jesus
Disciples 1, 2+
Martha
Mary

PROPS
Large pot and ladle
Dishes
Table
Chairs for Jesus and Disciples

THEMES
Faith, love for Jesus, prayer

COMMENTS
This story illustrates the primary place of faith in the life of a Christian. Martha invites Jesus to her house, but then is totally absorbed in the task of serving him and his companions. Meanwhile Mary, her sister, sits at the Lord's feet, listening to his teaching. Jesus chides Martha for her busy-ness, her anxiety, and worry. He teaches that focusing on him, as Mary is doing, is not only good but necessary. Valuing the person of Jesus and his message is the only thing that matters.

POINTS FOR DISCUSSION
• Friendship with Jesus

• Why Mary is praised
• The necessity of prayer
• How to pray centering prayer

PAYING TAXES TO CAESAR
||||||||||||||||||||||||||||||||||||||||||||||||||||||||||||||||||||||||||||||

Matthew 22:15-22   Mark 12:13-17
Luke 20:20-26
Twenty-Ninth Sunday of the Year A

CAST
Jesus
Pharisees 1, 2
Pharisees' Disciples 1, 2+
Crowd+

PROPS
Money bag
Coin

THEME
Obedience to law

COMMENTS
The Pharisees seek to trap Jesus in the matter of paying taxes. Beginning in A.D. 6, the Romans exacted from the Jewish people a census tax, which the Jewish people resented. The tax had to be paid by a silver Roman coin. If Jesus supported the tax, he would alienate his people. If he said the tax shouldn't be paid, his enemies could report him to the governor as a rebel, like a Zealot. Jesus escapes the trap by using his wit. Coins bore the image of the emperor and were inscribed "Tiberius Caesar, son of the Divine Augustus." They were his possession. Ironically, when Jesus asks for this coin, the Pharisees have one, though apparently Jesus does not. This means they already submit to the emperor themselves and use his system of commerce.

By saying "Give to Caesar the things that are Caesar's and to God the things that are God's," Jesus implies that loyalty to state and obedience to God need not contradict. It is up to us to apply this principle and determine what exactly belongs to "Caesar."

POINTS FOR DISCUSSION
- Why the question of the Pharisees was a trap
- The meaning and importance of obedience
- How to practice good citizenship

THE WOMAN CAUGHT IN ADULTERY

John 8:2-11
Fifth Sunday of Lent C

CAST	PROP
Narrator	Chair
Jesus	
Woman	
Scribes 1, 2+	
Pharisees 1, 2+	
Crowd+	

THEMES
Forgiveness, sinners, hypocrisy

COMMENTS
The Pharisees use a woman's humiliation to ensnare Jesus. Having caught her in adultery, they bring her to him and ask if she should be stoned. If Jesus answers "No," he will be contradicting the Law of Moses which prescribes death for her crime. If Jesus answers "Yes," he will depart from his own teaching of mercy. Jesus writes on the ground. What he writes and why he writes remain a mystery. One theory is that he was listing the sins of all those present.

Then Jesus cleverly invites those without sin to throw the first stone. Conscious of their sins and perhaps realizing how base was the trap they laid, the Pharisees disperse. In St. Augustine's words, "There remained together great misery and great mercy." Jesus, the sinless one, frees the woman, but with an admonition to sin no more. He gives her a chance to change her life.

POINTS FOR DISCUSSION
- The evil of hypocrisy and self-righteousness
- What Jesus could have written on the ground and why
- The willingness of Jesus to forgive
- How the sacrament of reconciliation brings Jesus' mercy to us
- How we can show mercy to others

ZACCHAEUS, THE TAX COLLECTOR

Luke 19:1-10
Thirty-First Sunday of the Year C

CAST	PROP
Narrator	Chair or ladder for tree
Jesus	
Zacchaeus	
Person	
Crowd+	

THEMES
Conversion, sinners, mission of Jesus

COMMENTS
Jesus demonstrates that it is possible for a rich man to be saved. Zacchaeus is a tax collector who collected taxes for the Roman oppressors. To the Jewish people, tax collector was synonymous with sinner. Being short, in order to see Jesus passing by, Zacchaeus climbs a sycamore tree, a tree with a short trunk and wide branches. When Jesus invites himself to Zacchaeus' house, the crowd objects. But Zacchaeus responds with joy. He is open to Jesus and his life is changed. He makes restitution for his sins far beyond what is necessary. His whole household reaps the benefits. This story clearly shows that Jesus seeks out sinners.

POINTS FOR DISCUSSION

- Ways that Jesus reaches out to Zacchaeus
- How Zacchaeus is open to salvation
- The importance of restitution and penance as a sign of conversion
- The call to go out to those who are outcasts
- How Jesus reaches out to us in different ways, especially by inviting us to Eucharist

THE WIDOW'S OFFERING

Mark 12:41-44   Luke 21:1-4
Thirty-Second Sunday of the Year B

CAST	PROPS
Narrator	Chair
Jesus	Large bowl for
Disciples 1, 2+	money
Wealthy Persons 1, 2+	Table for bowl
Widow	Bags of money
	Two small coins

THEMES

The poor, generosity, holiness

COMMENTS

In the Temple's Court of Women were thirteen horn-shaped chests for offerings, each labeled for a certain purpose. Jesus sits and watches people deposit money. A widow comes. She is one of the truly holy Jewish people who contrast with the righteous "pious ones." The widow puts in two copper coins, the smallest coins in circulation. Jesus praises her generosity because the coins were all she had. She didn't even keep one of the two coins for herself. Her offering was more than everyone else's, for she gave her total security. The story of the widow's offering leads into the story of Christ's offering. He, too, gave his all.

POINTS FOR DISCUSSION

- Why the widow's offering was great
- The obligation to give to the church
- What we can offer the church besides money
- The value of not being attached to possessions

THE ENTRY INTO JERUSALEM

Matthew 21:1-11   Mark 11:1-11
Luke 19:28-40   John 12:12-19
Passion Sunday (Procession) A, B, C

CAST	PROPS
Narrator	Chair, broom, or
Jesus	mop for colt
Disciples 1, 2, 3, 4+	Rope for colt
Bystander	Cloaks
Crowd+	Branches
Pharisees 1, 2+	
Person+	

THEMES

Identity of Jesus, humility

COMMENTS

Jesus enters Jerusalem as Messiah-king. He rides a colt because he is not a military Messiah, but a humble one. The people who know about his raising Lazarus from the dead acclaim him as king and Messiah. They hope for the restoration of David's kingdom. They strew branches on the ground to make it soft. They spread their cloaks, the red carpet treatment afforded royalty. They greet him with hosannas, a cry of acclamation that means "Do save us." The Pharisees fear that the procession might attract the notice of the Romans. But their attempts to quell the noisy crowd are futile. They admit that the whole world is following after Jesus.

POINTS FOR DISCUSSION
- The type of Messiah the people expected
- Characteristics of the kingdom of God
- The humility of Jesus
- What adoration is and why we adore God
- Why we receive palm branches on Passion Sunday and how to use them

THE LAST SUPPER

|||||||||||||||||||||||||||||||||||||||||||||||||||||||||||||||||||||||||||||||||||||||||||||||||||||||||||||||||||||||||||||||||||||||||||||

Matthew 26:20-29   Mark 14:17-26
Luke 22:14-22   John 13:1-27
Passion Sunday A, B, C
Holy Thursday A, B, C (Washing of Feet)

CAST	*PROPS*
Narrator	Table
Jesus	Bread
Twelve Apostles	Cup
	Bowl
	Robe for Jesus
	Basin
	Pitcher
	Towel

THEMES
Eucharist, service

COMMENTS
The earliest record of the institution of the Eucharist is in 1 Corinthians 11:23-25. In John's account of the Last Supper, the washing of the feet is described, but not the institution of the Eucharist. The washing is a parable in action of what the Eucharist stands for. By assuming the role of the lowest, Jesus shows his disciples how they are to love one another. The four gospel accounts of the Last Supper differ in other details. In the gospels of Matthew and Mark, Judas' betrayal occurs before the Eucharist, but in Luke and John, Judas shares the meal with Jesus.

By the time of Jesus, the Jewish people had adapted the Hellenistic custom of eating while reclining on carpets and pillows around a low table. The diners shared large bowls in the center. It is supposed that the Last Supper was the Passover meal. Blessing of the bread and distributing it and the drinking of wine is part of that Jewish ritual. The paschal lamb is the symbol of Christ, the unblemished victim of the sin of humankind. As at the Passover meal, after sharing the bread and wine, Jesus, as presider, explains their meaning. Unlike at the Passover meal, the bread is his body and the wine, his blood. He is inaugurating a covenant. Just as covenants of the Hebrew Scriptures were ratified by sprinkling the blood of the sacrificed animal over the people, Jesus seals his new covenant with his blood—the symbol of life. He is the new Passover victim.

POINTS FOR DISCUSSION
- The humility and love of Jesus
- What Jesus asks of his disciples
- Why we celebrate the Eucharist
- The parts of the celebration of Mass today
- How to participate in the Eucharist fully

THE AGONY IN THE GARDEN

Matthew 26:36-56   Mark 14:32-52
Luke 22:39-53   John 18:1-12
Passion Sunday A, B, C

CAST

Narrator
Jesus
Eleven Apostles
Judas
Soldiers+
Malchus

PROPS

Swords

THEMES

Prayer, mission of Jesus, obedience, suffering of Jesus

COMMENTS

The garden Jesus and his apostles go to was probably the private garden of a friend. Jesus takes the favored three and then leaves them to pray by himself. He is overwhelmed by sorrow. He asks that the Father take the cup of suffering away from him, but submits to his plan. People retired early in those days, and the apostles fall asleep in the garden instead of being a comfort to Jesus. They are a symbol of those who are not alert to their final test. When the Temple soldiers come to arrest Jesus and Peter tries to prevent them, Jesus stops him. It is the hour now for the climactic struggle between God and Satan.

The kiss of Judas is a normal Near East greeting. Here it serves to identify Jesus in the dark and becomes a symbol of betrayal.

POINTS FOR DISCUSSION

• Ways the humanity of Jesus is shown
• Obedience to God
• Praying at crucial times
• The value of self-denial
• How we can betray Jesus or be loyal to him

THE TRIAL BEFORE PILATE

Mark 15:1-20   Matthew 27:11-31
Luke 23:1-25   John 18:28-19:16
Passion Sunday A, B, C
Good Friday A, B, C

CAST

Narrator
Jesus
Pilate
Soldiers 1, 2, 3, 4+
Jewish Leaders 1, 2+
Messenger

PROPS

Cloak
Crown of thorns
Chair
Bowl

THEMES

Identity of Jesus, suffering of Jesus, death of Jesus

COMMENTS

Jesus' trial before Pilate focuses on his innocence and on his identity. The dream of Pilate's wife and the handwashing occur only in Matthew's account. They underline the innocence of Jesus. The Scripture authors make the Jewish leaders, not Rome, responsible for the death of Jesus. The leaders bring Jesus to Pilate because they do not have the power to crucify. In choosing to free the Zealot, Barabbas (whose name means Son of the Father), over Jesus, they are choosing political liberation rather than the true Messiah.

Gospels portray Pilate as fickle and subservient to the Jewish crowd. History, on the other hand, tells us that Pilate was strong-willed and held the Jewish people in contempt. In the gospels, although Pilate finds Jesus without blame, he gives in to the pressure of the Jewish crowd when his career is threatened.

Jesus is drawn as Messiah and king during the trial. The charge against him is that he said that he was king of the Jews. This claim amounts to treason against Rome, a capital offense. Jesus explains to Pilate that his kingdom is not of this world. In the end, the Roman soldiers mock him as king. They put a crown of thorns on him and a cloak, which was probably the scarlet cloak of the Roman soldiers. Ironically, these Gentiles unwittingly do homage to their real king as he is about to give his life for them and for all his people.

Scourging before crucifixion was routine procedure for the Romans. It was a terrible ordeal performed with a whip of leather strips ending in knots or bits of metal or bone. After this torture, Jesus is led to his throne, the cross.

POINTS FOR DISCUSSION
- The dignity of Jesus during the trial
- The sufferings Jesus endured for us
- Why Pilate ordered Jesus crucified
- In what sense Jesus was a king
- The Stations of the Cross
- What part we played in the suffering and death of Jesus
- How we can thank Jesus for being our Savior

THE RESURRECTION

John 20:1-18
Easter Sunday A, B, C

CAST
Narrator
Jesus
Peter
John
Mary
Angels 1, 2

PROPS
Two cloths

THEMES
Resurrection, women, Peter, love for Jesus

COMMENTS
No one witnessed the actual resurrection. The first clue that Jesus is risen is the empty tomb. All the gospels record that before dawn women came to the tomb. Although John focuses on Mary Magdalene (or Mary of Magdala), her use of "we" indicates that she was with others. John lets Peter enter the tomb first. Peter, therefore, predominates in the story. The apostles see the burial cloths. The wrapping for the head is rolled up and separate. This probably means that it was still in the oval shape it took when it was looped around the head and knotted at the top to keep the jaw from slacking. The presence of the linens discredits the rumor that the body was stolen. Thieves would not leave the wrappings behind. The disciples do not understand the full impact of the scene. They have yet to receive the Holy Spirit.

It is fitting that Mary Magdalene, who faithfully stood at the cross, is the first to see the risen Lord. But because he is so altered in his glorified state or because her vision is so blurred from tears, she mistakes him for the gardener. Her love for Jesus prompts her to ask where the body is so that she can take it. She is oblivious to whether or not she can do this. Mary recognizes Jesus immediately when he says her name. She calls him "Rabbouni," a form of rabbi. Jesus tells Mary to stop clinging to him. He still must return to the Father and complete the cycle of his glorification and our salvation.

POINTS FOR DISCUSSION
- The evidence of Jesus' resurrection
- How Jesus is the same and yet different
- The deep love of Mary Magdalene for Jesus
- The deference John shows to Peter
- What difference the resurrection makes for us

THE APPEARANCE TO THE WOMEN

|||||||||||||||||||||||||||||||||||||||||||||||||||||||||||||||||||||||||||||||||||||||||||||||||||

Matthew 28:1-10   Mark 16:1-8
Luke 24:1-12
Easter Vigil A, B, C

CAST   *PROPS*
Narrator   Bags (for spices)
Angel   Chair for rock
Mary
Women 1, 2
Guards+
Disciples 1, 2+
Peter
Jesus

THEMES
Resurrection, women, Peter

COMMENTS
The women are going to anoint Jesus' body. As an afterthought, they wonder how they will move the heavy, flat stone that covers the entrance to the tomb. Their worries are allayed when the stone is moved for them. The women are full of fear on seeing the angel and the empty tomb. The details in this account of the resurrection highlight the glory of the event: the angel, the dazzling white cloths, the earthquake, the fainting guards. The disbelief of the disciples is understandable. In Mark and Luke, Peter is singled out as the one who learns of the resurrection. Interestingly, it is women who are the first heralds of the resurrection, not the apostles.

POINTS FOR DISCUSSION
• Why there were guards at the tomb
• Signs of the resurrection
• Why the disciples do not believe
• How to live if we believe in the resurrection

THE APPEARANCE
ON THE EMMAUS ROAD

|||||||||||||||||||||||||||||||||||||||||||||||||||||||||||||||||||||||||||||||||||||||||||||||||||

Luke 24:13-35
Third Sunday of Easter A

CAST   *PROPS*
Narrator   Table
Jesus   Three chairs
Cleopas   Bread
Disciple

THEMES
Resurrection, identity of Jesus, Eucharist

COMMENTS
The Emmaus story is the story of all people who come to know Jesus. Two disciples are leaving Jerusalem with their hopes dashed. One is identified as Cleopas; the other could be his wife. They had hoped that Jesus was the Messiah, but are discouraged by his death. When Jesus comes to them, not recognizing him, they summarize the good news for him. He dispels their confusion and doubts by explaining how the Scriptures foretell that the Messiah would have to suffer. When the travelers reach Emmaus, about seven miles from Jerusalem, the two disciples invite Jesus to stay with them. During supper as Jesus is breaking bread, they suddenly realize who he is. He vanishes and they immediately return to Jerusalem to tell the other disciples what happened.

This account has the structure of the eucharistic liturgy. First the disciples hear the word, and then they share a meal with Christ. In the Eucharist, Jesus is present with his people no less than he was before his death.

POINTS FOR DISCUSSION
• The difference in Jesus that kept the disciples from recognizing him
• The importance of the Scriptures in learning our faith

- The significance of the Eucharist for Christians
- Ways Jesus is present in the eucharistic celebration

THE APPEARANCE TO THE APOSTLES

Luke 24:36-51
Third Sunday of Easter B
Pentecost A, B, C

CAST	PROPS
Narrator	Table
Jesus	Fish
Disciples 1, 2+	

THEMES
Resurrection, evangelization, good news, ministry

COMMENTS
The disciples experience the resurrected Jesus as a human being. He assures them he was not a ghost. He shows them his wounds, asks for food, and eats fish in front of them. Eating was an understood sign that someone was not a ghost. Jesus is able to eat just as the daughter of Jairus had been able to eat.

The disciples move from shock, confusion, and fear to peace and joy. Jesus recalls how he had told them about the closing events of his life on earth and how the Scriptures pointed to them. He foretells that they will witness these things and preach repentance to all nations. It is the promised Spirit who will make things clear to the disciples and empower them to carry out their mission.

POINTS FOR DISCUSSION
- Characteristics of a glorified body
- Why the apostles were afraid
- How Jesus identified himself
- How to carry out our responsibility to evangelize

THE APPEARANCE TO THOMAS

John 20:19-29
Second Sunday of Easter A, B, C

CAST
Narrator
Jesus
Disciples +
Thomas

THEMES
Resurrection, forgiveness, faith, the Spirit

COMMENTS
Jesus was truly resurrected. His entering through locked doors showed that he had not merely survived crucifixion. He had died and risen. He possessed new spiritual qualities. Jesus is, however, the same person the disciples knew and loved. The wounds in his hands and feet identify him. Jesus' first word to his disciples was "Shalom," that is, "Peace be with you." Understandably he had to calm their fears. Not only were the disciples seeing a person they knew had died, but someone almost all of them had abandoned.

Jesus' breathing on his disciples was a sign of the giving of his Spirit. Breath signifies life. The Spirit of creation brings us new life. Now that Jesus is risen, the Spirit will empower his church to carry on his mission. His disciples will share in his power to forgive and to reconcile the world through the sacraments. They, too, will bring peace.

Thomas comes to believe that the Lord is risen not on the words of others but by his own eyes. He makes a great act of faith. He calls Jesus "Lord" and "God," terms that were used for the name of the God of Israel. Unlike Thomas' faith, our faith depends not on sight, but on the gospel, the Word.

POINTS OF DISCUSSION

- Why the apostles needed peace
- The gift of the sacrament of reconciliation
- How we can arrive at faith
- Some things we find hard to believe

SUNDAY AND FEAST-DAY GOSPELS
CONTAINING THE PLAYS IN THIS BOOK

Playlets can help prepare the students to celebrate Sunday and feast-day liturgies. The gospels of the following days are about events that are the subject of a playlet in this book.

LITURGY	*EVENT*
Second Sunday of Advent A, B, C	The Baptism of Jesus (John the Baptist)
Third Sunday of Advent B	
Third Sunday of Advent C	
Fourth Sunday of Advent B	The Annunciation
Fourth Sunday of Advent C	The Visitation
Christmas Mass at Midnight A, B, C	The Birth of Jesus
Chrismas Mass at Dawn A, B, C	The Birth of Jesus
January 1, Octave of Christmas, Solemnity of Mary, Mother of God	The Birth of Jesus
Sunday in the Octave of Christmas B	The Presentation
Sunday in the Octave of Christmas C	The Boy Jesus in the Temple
Epiphany A, B, C	The Visit of the Magi
Sunday after January 6 A, B, C	The Baptism of Jesus
First Sunday of Lent A, B, C	The Temptation of Jesus
Second Sunday of Lent A, B, C	The Transfiguration of Jesus
Third Sunday of Lent A	The Samaritan Woman
Third Sunday of Lent B	The Cleansing of the Temple
Fifth Sunday of Lent C	The Woman Caught in Adultery
Passion Sunday (Procession) A, B, C	The Entry into Jerusalem
Passion Sunday A, B, C	The Last Supper
	The Agony in the Garden
	The Trial Before Pilate
Passion Sunday B	The Anointing at Bethany
Holy Thursday A, B, C	The Last Supper (Washing of the Feet)
Good Friday A, B, C	The Trial Before Pilate
Easter Vigil A, B, C	The Appearance to the Women
Easter Sunday A, B, C	The Resurrection
Second Sunday of Easter A, B, C	The Appearance to Thomas
Third Sunday of Easter A	The Appearance on the Emmaus Road
Third Sunday of Easter B	The Appearance to the Apostles
Pentecost A, B, C	The Appearance to the Apostles
Second Sunday of the Year B	The First Apostles
Third Sunday of the Year B	The Call of the First Apostles

INDEX OF THEMES

The following topics can be enlivened by a playlet in this book.